Democracy's
Second Chance

Democracy's Second Chance

LAND, WORK AND
CO-OPERATION

by

GEORGE BOYLE

1941

SHEED & WARD

NEW YORK

To

V. D. SCHAFFNER, M.D., F.A.C.S.

Contents

Acknowledgments

To Dr. J. J. Tompkins through whose stimulation and advice this book came to be written; to Dr. M. M. Coady for his teachings in Co-operation; to St. Francis Xavier University, Antigonish, Nova Scotia, through whose Extension Department conditions of study were provided; to various co-operative business leaders throughout the Maritime Provinces from whom the author learned a great deal; and finally to Miss Zita O'Hcarn and Miss Margaret McDonald for their work in retyping the script. The author is solely responsible for the views set forth in this book.

G. B.

Permissions

The author desires to express his gratitude to the following for permissions to use excerpts from the books or articles indicated:

ALLIANCE BOOK CORPORATION, publishers of Herman Rauschning's *The Revolution of Nihilism.*

DODD, MEAD & COMPANY, publishers of *Orthodoxy* by G. K. Chesterton.

DUTTON & CO., INC., publishers of *Unto This Last* by John Ruskin; also to EVERYMAN'S LIBRARY for same.

JOHN STEVENS, Newport, R. I., publisher of *Work and Culture* by Eric Gill.

THE MACMILLAN COMPANY, publishers of *A Memoir of AE* by John Eglinton.

The magazine FORTUNE for quotation from article on Farm Income in its issue of October 1937.

The magazine RURAL AMERICA for quotations from articles by Dr. Jacob Lange and by Murray D. Lincoln.

Foreword

by A. B. MacDonald

St. Francis Xavier University Extension Dept., Antigonish, N. S.

For many years the trend of population towards the city has been irresistible and disturbing. It is seen in almost all countries of the Western World. The point is widely emphasized that many of our social ills are associated with this trend, and it becomes clearer that we cannot solve our social problems until we come to grips with it.

Although technological and scientific advances have made it possible to satisfy more and more of the material needs of man, somehow the tiller of the soil has not benefited to any great extent from the inventions of the past seventy-five years. The majority of farmers have failed to profit from the discovery of new techniques even in agriculture itself. The farm home is still without most of the ordinary conveniences of life. Rural youth lacks the educational advantages available in the city. Rural people have had taken from them the great heritage of the crafts, the liberating skills of home-use production: the vision and the techniques to put into effect that degree of self-sufficiency which the endowment of their terrain permits. The lonely struggle for a meager livelihood has tended to obscure in the mind of the farmer the great possibilities of group action for his social, economic and cultural development.

Public leaders, recognizing the plight of agriculture,

have for many decades been carrying on educational work designed to promote a greater degree of security and contentment for rural people. Agricultural colleges and experimental stations have been established. Extension workers from departments of agriculture and universities have spent much money and effort in the rehabilitation of agriculture. Churchmen and educators have consistently pointed out the advantages of country life in comparison with urban life. Yet the problem of a waning countryside and of a disheartened rural people is as acute as ever. It is true that some progress has been made. If the enlightening and energizing forces of these agencies had not been at work, rural conditions would be far worse.

Nevertheless we must be humble enough to ask ourselves: Wherein have we failed? Have we yet discovered the proper combination of factors—educational, economic, cultural and spiritual—which will make for a self-reliant and creative living on the land? Obviously some essential dynamic is lacking in our rural philosophy and program.

The mechanization of industry which has been throwing out of employment thousands of workers each year, and the present trend to decentralism, make it all the more urgent that we discover the missing factor in our rural life. It may be that in the past we have been accustomed to think too much of mechanical power and too little of what someone has called "the little green powers." At any rate, in this book Mr. Boyle presents some new and challenging ideas that should help to clarify our thinking on the rural question. He makes it clear that in approaching its solution we must be prepared to re-examine our whole scale of human value.

George Boyle is no mere theorist about rural life. He was born on a farm and has lived, through several periods of his life, in the country. In his own lifetime and in his own native land he has observed the disintegrating forces that are everywhere undermining the oldest and most vital avocation of man. He has consistently expressed his views on the subject in *The Extension Bulletin* and *The Maritime Co-operator*.

Never has there been such a searching examination of our whole social and economic system as we see today. Never before has there been such unanimity among public men on the importance of life on the land in the social order that is to come. For this reason both city and rural people will find Mr. Boyle's work timely and stimulating.

PART I

Ideas and Attitudes That Underlie Rural Life

CHAPTER I

The Flight from the Land

IN 1880 the population of the United States was 71 per cent rural. This means that 71 persons out of 100 lived in the open country, or in villages and towns numbering up to, but not above, 2,500 souls. These towns themselves were natural centers of rural activity. By 1930 the people classed as rural had dropped to 43 per cent. By 1935 only 25 per cent of the United States population were actually living on farms. With the migration of people went the migration of wealth. Migration from the farm from 1920 to 1929 in the United States, according to O. F. Baker, took into the towns more than twelve and one half billion dollars.[1]

It is safe to say that the greater part of such wealth tends to become invested in industries and services extractive of further profits from the farm population. Rural life, the natural place for average men and average families to work out their salvation, becomes down-at-heel and apologetic. Young rural people affected by the bled-out condition of their environment join the job-seekers in the already overbuilt urban structures. Worst of all, the piling up of wealth in the towns and cities through its influence on the instruments of enlightenment and culture creates an anti-rural bias, keeps up a constant apologetic of its own standards, suppresses a whole scale of values associated with rural

[1] *Agriculture and Modern Life*, O. F. Baker. New York, Harper and Brothers, 1939.

living, and nurtures a type of citizen who is so preoccupied with holding his own in the economic melee
that he remains unaware of the cumulus of forces that
consolidate poverty.

The cityward slide of populations has been common
to all countries involved in centralized industrialism.
In Canada the slide has been roughly in proportion to
that of the United States. The Dominion Bureau of
Statistics gives to the term *rural* a more restricted meaning. But the trend, made so obvious by abandoned
farms, by over-populated towns and cities with their
hard core of unemployment and the general air of
transiency and frustration, hardly needs the sharp re-
proach of statistics. The population trend briefly
glimpsed is this:

	Rural	*Urban*
1881........	3,215,303	1,109,507
1931........	4,804,728	5,572,058

For an unfilled country like Canada the urbanizing
trend is of special significance. With a small population according to our age and area, we enter blindly
into conditions of further decline. City birth-rates are
low. To state it most indulgently, we are courting the
danger of becoming stunted in our youth rather than
static in middle age as with some more populous lands.

For a long time the French Canadian showing was
a record of rapid increase. Dr. Egbert Munzer gives
this analysis of the trend.

"The first reliable census is that of 1763. At that
time the land along the St. Lawrence River and the

little settlements in the hinterland had a population of 65,000 practically all of French descent.

"Since that time immigration from France has been negligible, a consequence of the country becoming British in 1759. Only during the last decades before 1914 there was some additional immigration, but it is, for our purposes, of no avail since the time is too short to allow for a greater reproduction of this—by the way negligible—part of French immigration.

"According to the census of 1931, the number of French reached the figure of 2,927,990. But this is not all. The United States census of 1930 shows that 370,852 French Canadians born in Canada, lived in the United States and that 735,307 native-born Americans had at least one French Canadian parent.

"In other words, in about six generations the 65,000 French Canadians had multiplied to nearly *four million*. That means that in every generation the French Canadians have doubled their number. In actual fact, during the first 100 years of this era, from 1760 to 1860, the rate of increase was far higher than after 1860; after that date the process of urbanization and other reasons mostly connected with this phenomenon, made the very high reproduction-rate of the French Canadians fall severely. The percentage of rural population in the Province of Quebec, e.g., has decreased from 77.2 in 1871 to 36.9 in 1931.

"The French Canadians are the most striking example of a race which during its rural existence showed a very great increase. If the French of France would have increased in a similar ratio, France would have reached by now a population of about 600 million. It equally shows that the urbanization is the death of any nation; even such a vigorous race as the French Canadians loses its high birth-rate if it begins to flock into the big cities. The present birth-rate of the French Canadians is about 24 as against 19 of the Federal average. The fertility of the purely rural French population has remained high. The city kills the nations."

The urban drift, and the scale of values which it sets up, creates the labor problem. A solution of the labor and social question, of unemployment, the bread-line, relief, nihilist employment, overcrowded cities cannot be reached without re-discovery of the land and the re-establishment of a scale of values human and organic. The debris of centralism, that concentration of uprooted population, of industry and of what passes for culture, becomes a more deadening weight as time goes on. As the flame draws the moth, unopposed centralism draws out-lying populations into its enfeeblement. It becomes a mania. Rational values are given over for a sense of togetherness. The person puts aside the qualitative in order to avail himself of the forces that swell from the massed volumes of humanity.

This does not mean that there should not be centers. To imply that would be tantamount to desiring anarchy. But in truth a center is no longer a center when it becomes over-centralized. It then sins by an excess of its own principle. The modern city takes on the qualities of both the parasite and the octopus. More than 2,000 years ago, Plato, consulting history up to the time, found that societies and civilizations had perished by excess of their own principles. The same process is at work all through history.

A center is only a center when it maintains the decentralizing processes. The heart is the blood-center of the human body, driving life out into the extremities. What is really good is diffusive of itself.

The restoration of balance between town and country is a necessary activity in the return of reason and Christianity. We were closer to this in the Middle Ages, though even then the problem existed. In the pre-industrial era, towns were natural centers of rural cultures. Young people from the rural areas came to the towns to learn the crafts and to get their education, then returned to their home communities taking with them the lights of learning and leadership. This was decentralist culture and economics. This was germane to Christianity which, though one in its thought, was decentralist in its works, as is evidenced by its constant missionary activity.

Mass production, with its attendant commercialism and in particular the influence which the latter had on culture, inverted this. Educated people, and people with qualities of leadership, no longer took back the life-blood into the outlands. Instead, they hung out their shingles in the towns, or better still in the cities; and the bigger the city the better, so they thought, as it made one feel more important. It is commonly admitted that while it is better to live in the country one feels more important in the city. That is probably true. To live in the reflected ferment of the collectivity is the easiest possible way to compensate for inner emptiness. The emptier you are, the bigger the place to which you should go. Modern urbanism is already an ill-visaged collectivism. And, as Marx saw, the frustrated class in the towns and cities, the proletariat, becomes a very usable tool for revolutionary activities, titanic forces in the hands of tyrants.

The social problem is an agrico-social problem. There needs to be a rebirth of localism in all phases. The decentralist process is the most wholesome possible for the towns and cities.

Why people leave the land to become proletarians has been a subject of speculation. There are many different tints and attractions to the mirage of urbanism that has drawn populations towards illusory goals. People leave the land because they feel unable to function in important and satisfying fields of endeavor as agrarians. Rural life has lost its self-respect. On this continent there has been no continuity of rural culture. The beginning made by the early generations had not had time to flower when swept aside by the pride and bombast of the cities. Industrialism, the rise of the bourgeois spirit, the total surrender to the unchallenged standards of a seller's culture emptied the land of its vital and creative human elements. Rural life became conscious of itself only to become ashamed of itself. The small farmer became apologetic. Rural living was something only to be endured. The vital spirit was gone. The machine had routed the organism.

In studying the material bases of rural life the key word is *organism*. I use the word in its true sense of the thing which has life, the thing which possesses either the vegetative or the animal soul, the mysterious principle which is beyond the ken of the scientist, and which is thereby distinguished from mechanisms and inanimate matter. Three powers has the organism: nutrition, growth and reproduction. In these energies is the enormous cavalcade of the living.

Like the organism, the whole reason and reality of a provident rural culture—the crafts, home-use production, husbandry—were largely swept aside. Whole sets of rural skills, knowledge and attitudes were lost. The idea of culture changed. The wage-earner who made enough money to engage in "conspicuous consumption" of mass-produced goods came on the stage. That he was dependent upon an employer mattered not. He replaced the artisan who expressed the artist in man, and who could resort to self-employment and found in creative personal work the satisfactions that the mere employee had to take out in conspicuous consumption.

Between the wage-earner who aims at engaging in conspicuous consumption of economic goods as a norm of culture and the artisan in man expressing himself in personal responsible work that provides the man with basic necessities of living there is an important difference. The former is Economic Man at his most reckless. Peter Drucker sees the passing of Economic Man;[2] he succumbs to non-economic hierarchies in the army-states of totalitarian fascism, and his passing marks the end of an era in human history. On the contrary, the latter is man at his most responsible, most free and fully human. The farmer-artisan is the prototype of the decentralist state.

[2] *The End of Economic Man,* Peter Drucker. The John Day Company, New York, 1939.

The industrial revolution, with its headlong confusion of technical expediency with true progress, has initiated the slave state. The conditions for the turning-away from the fascinations of the machine towards a rational use of the machine are ripening.

We need to state all the reasons why rural life (not the primitive, isolated community) is good. There can be brought back to view slighted and forgotten truths. What we have forgotten through the industrial revolution is, perchance, more important than what we have remembered. We have been preoccupied with mechanical forces, we have not thought much of organic forces—the biological investiture of earth: those carriers of LIFE and fellow-travelers of man down through the un-measured ages—the animals and plants in all their myriad sub-species. From this organic community urban and industrial man seeks to depart. The flight is the flight from the living.

The machine, carried out of bounds by the greed of capitalism and now seized by the tyrants as the effective engine of domination, bestows this trait upon its victims: It blinds them to the obvious; its irrational use drives them on in endless motion which acts against the meditative and perceptive capacities. Man tends to become a mere passenger riding about on sub-cosmic forces. The mechanist and the materialist receive the full indemnity of their half-truth by being condemned to believe it and go through life as servants of the physical properties of matter.

The machine is its own propaganda. By its noise and its glitter and its delivering from drudgery it has fascinated. The economy of attention is a law of the mind and it operates against man's being able to keep an objective attitude towards the machine. Only by a conscious effort, by a re-mustering of the meditative in man, can machine nihilism be perceived, not to say resisted. The machine has come to its ultimate dynamism in the slave state, to the controls of which gravitate seekers of power. Against dependence on such, every lover of freedom must be interested in a new heraldry of the organic power: the unsung praise and power of the organism.

This, it will be seen, is a turning to life itself, to mystery and to spirit. For every last thing that lives has some sort of soul. All the colossal cavalcade that comes forward from Genesis has in it some spark from the breath of the Eternal. This, the mighty drama of the living!

The mechanist is blind to Genesis contemporaneous. He is cut off from the sustaining arm and vision of life. The countryman senses deeply the drama, because of his companioning with animals and plants, with insect and bird, with microbe and weed, with the organisms at their best and worst. But his feeling is mostly instinctive. And when he has been influenced by modern education it is apt to become apologetic; for modern education, given over to urban standards at its fountain-heads, has not upheld the nobility of the organic principle, has not uncovered its social significance, has appeared to be totally ignorant of the relation between the organic rhythm and the psychic states of man.

A full rural philosophy has never been stated. We

have not had a rural philosophy stated as comprehensively as the Marxist philosophy, for instance, though this is a man-betraying cult. In fact, the materialistic theory of society co-exists with ignorance of the organic foundations of life. The industrial cities, the rise of the great wage-class and of the proletariat marked a turning from the organic principle which is the material base of rural life and which gives to rural life its distinctive character. Before Marx, industrialism under the bourgeois spirit had laid the conditions of materialism: these later-day tyrannies of technical force are the natural issue. In being placed in an environment of mechanism, of metallic and naked material, and being cut off from contact with the life-continuity of organisms, the worker becomes easily a mechanist and in world-outlook—a materialist.

The peasant is never a materialist. He may be a pagan. But he always has some kind of gods. In his materials of livelihood he is dealing too closely with some kind of active spirit to be an unbeliever. The materialism of the things that, although material, have the evidences of spirit within them, the organic things, offset the gross materialism of the mechanist. Here is a possible basis for the dissolution of the materialist world. In the predominantly rural environment man has all about him the handicraft of spirit. Subconsciously he comes to know his kinship. Even the fairy tales of the peasant are often closer to ultimate reality than the short-based, brittle, bitter logic of men whom the machine environment has made materialists.

The machine was not the whole story. In the wake of

mass production grew up the seller's culture, harrowing
the souls of the masses with new and often artificial
wants. The insecurity of workpeople which came as a
result of separation from the provident if frugal organic
bases helped strengthen greed and dishonesty. There
is no one more greedy than the insecure man. He has
to be. Business is business, it is said. This means, in
short: soak the other fellow because some other fellow
is out to soak you. For the most part the seller's culture
is one that uses greed, trickery, competition, lies, delu-
sion and dishonesty as the very minimum instruments
of survival. It lives by its wits. For the most part this
type of culture remains unexposed, nay, it remains the
unchallenged norm and having surrendered to gadgets
and mere externals is incapable of entertaining any
patterns but its own. It is in this that the provincialism
of the urban mind has risen. Before its imperious assumption of its own superiority the brightest rural
youth abandon all idea of the possibility of a rural culture. The farmer's brightest son becomes a bank clerk,
a salesman or a merchant.

It is not upon persons or upon the class that blame
is to be laid. It is upon the standards. And for these
standards we are all jointly to blame. We are all victims
of the dominant spirit of the culture of our age. The rise
of mercantilism, not only as a trade system but also as
one of the dominants in thought, was to serve standards
that had already begun to throw undue emphasis on
the economic. Production for use gave way to production for sale. Upon this latter has been built what may
be termed a seller's culture. We are all brokers of some

sort; and even though we recognize the havoc around us we are powerless to break with the system, especially if we stay in the cities.[3]

The Christians, the Socialists and the believers in consumer's co-operation hold to the primacy of production for use. But they have not all insisted that, as to the simple necessities of life, production for use is at its best on the family farm. Rural life is the true arena for the production-for-use consciousness that is becoming clearer. It is the view of this writer that there cannot be a successful land movement of such a size as to help against unemployment without replacement of the seller's culture with what we shall term a provident culture: the bases of this latter to be land, crafts and co-operatives.

The slow stride and the guileless manner of the countryman speak of another life. His union with the organic principle permits a way of life that is freer from the sharpened trickeries of the marketplace. While he could hold on to his land this very security could have been a proper base for a culture of his own, had not the modern mind sold out to business and failed to bring him a culture of his own. It should have been possible for him, had he received a little help, to remain

[3] While landward development cannot be expected to flower without deflation of the success ideal—which seems entrenched in present-day education—it would be a mistake to direct ill-will against persons or classes. George Russell wrote:

"If an individual, ignoring the wise warning of the Gospels, condemns any one over much, what he condemns is meted out to him. If he says some one is very vain, vanity blooms all over him as he speaks, for the remark implies that the speaker believes he is stainless so far as this fault is concerned. If he says some one else is a most irritable person, he grows irritated himself, and so on through the whole range of emotions." *Co-operation and Nationality.*

free from the standardizations of cynicism. Stuart Chase
compares the character types:

> "Compare, let us say, a thousand assorted pioneers
> of the Berkshire Hills in Massachusetts in 1800 with
> a thousand assorted bank clerks in 1930, and, unless
> the monumental history of the Berkshires which I
> have lately ingested is a tissue of falsehoods, you will
> find about as many no men in the former area as
> you will find yes men in the latter. The ratios, I
> should guess, have reversed themselves in one hun-
> dred and thirty years. With the no men will lie
> character, courage, individuality, saltiness. With the
> yes men will lie radios, automobiles, bathtubs, and
> a complete paralysis of the will to act in accordance
> with their fundamental inclinations. . . .
> "From servants it is a long drop downward to the
> salesman, though here again we note, or are begin-
> ning to note, a loss of human dignity which is freez-
> ing into convention. It is the salesman's business to
> be hypocritical if necessary, just as it is the servant's
> business to be servile." [4]

On such well prepared ground the Marxist cynicism
could shake the world. The great gaping loophole in
the Marxist front, and in the whole materialist front
that has succeeded it, is that both were mechanist and
technical and presumed this trend to be irresistible.
But the trend has proved itself depletive, destructive
of men, and in fact not even good materialism. The
conditions of industrialism were necessary for the forg-

[4] *The Nemesis of American Business,* The Macmillan Co., New York,
1931.

ing of their bonds. To it belonged chains as of the proletariat. Even in their materialism they were blind, for they under-valued the animated materialisms of organic life. It was the denial of soul that came out of rationalism.

Ultimately the politics of centralized industry is statism. Basically it is on the organic principle that the foundations of liberty rest. Between these two poles oscillates the figure of man. Shall we in North America wait for lost liberties in the future to teach us that there is a power endowed beyond all things technical, a gentle power yet conquering the ages, a power which the botanist knows as the *appalling fecundity of earth?*

CHAPTER II

Power Is in the Organic

THROUGH the age of the rise of mechanisms—whose proper use is a blessing—people in the processes of being urbanized lost appreciation of the organic endowment of earth. But man has some indestructible affinity with mother earth and her brood. I have heard a sick man say poignantly, after having spent two years bedfast in a hospital: "My God, if I could but lie down once on the grass before I die." Likewise the city child knows his affinity with the green world and all little living things. He revels in all that lies about him in the country because his vision yet unspoiled sees the surprising truths of creation. He recognizes this drama of the living provisionment of earth. His sight is the true sight. The non-recognition of natural history and of the sacredness of life—of things that live—is one of the blanks in the adult sophisticated urban mind.

The machine or technical age has thought in terms of power. The imagination of workers and of the labor people has been taken up with turbines, with dynamos, with the concentrations of power and apparatus in industrial plants. Such forms of power inspire awe and thereby set up the mental conditions for enslavement. They shut out the tremendous fact that there are, in a certain authentic sense, more perfect forms of power.

I use *power* in the sense of a means to supply man's basic wants. Great size and volume are not the principles of excellence in power. Fundamentally and *socially* the first attribute of power is availability to men *without loss of freedom*. This is not present in the concentrated forms of technical power; in technical power the common man is dependent first on something in the mind of the technician, and second on the financier. Considering man's dignity, the perfect thing in power is that it be man-size—not corporation-size. This perfection is in organic power.

For an era steeped in ideas of power, are we not singularly blind about one of the most perfect, varied and ubiquitous forms of power in the world? As to his foodstuffs and basic necessities, the farmer is dependent not so much on any man or group but on this objective principle of earth's fecundity. On this primal fact rests the strength and honor of the profession. Properly to esteem rural life we must seek to understand the powers of the organic in its social and philosophical significance —not merely as crops and animals.

The more one examines the concept of power the more one sees that the ideal is to be adequate, yet small enough to be free of danger; productive, yet not enslaving; tenacious, yet not tyrannical. In the technical distortion since the rise of industrial capitalism we feel the need of socializing certain industries and rightly so —when the power is such that it is too dangerous to be in the hands of individuals. Do we stop to think that organic power was socialized by the Creator? Organic power is an external force, is everywhere, and yields free for the tending. By no edict of the state does the grain ripen or the grass send up its shoots. Organic power is freer than that, yet is designed, parceled out, apportioned down in forms beyond the counting and is usable by the commonest man. The organic power is the free and distributed power. It is socially integrated power. It is resilient. It is repletive. It is under the law of increase through natural reproduction. It incorporates the amazing actuality of being mighty and at the same time being delicate. Refinement of power par excellence it is—the mighty minutiae of the organic order.

"We have had dinned into our ears in the past twenty years a great deal about the Romance of industry and big business; we have become fascinated with power in the mechanized sense; we have lost sight of the romance and drama of organic life; we have almost lost the vision of the productive power that lies hidden in the organism as manifested in unnumbered forms in the plant and animal kingdoms and associated with life on the land. Here are the great faucets of abounding life renewed each year. Here is an arena of liberty, variety and adventure. Here is a new frontier of science. Here is work for all.

"Mechanized power with all its glitter has one great weakness—it is not available to the common man without taking a great toll in money and liberty. It is not socially integrated power.

"Organic power is socially integrated power: the potatoes will sprout, the wheat will ripen, the hens will lay as faithfully for the poor man as for the rich man. Such as these and a thousand others constitute a source of power, allotted, fitted, and available to the hand of the common man. But how many see this? And it is vitally necessary that people going on the land should see it.

"When clergymen and scientists and philosophers and poets begin to lead the people to these fountain-heads of material sustenance we may expect a new and better day. The emphasis in the recent past has been away from these things." [1]

To say that organic power is repletive seems a simple phrase, to be easily passed over by a generation of noise-worshipers. But it is a distinction so colossal that it is more than a distinction; it is also a direction. It marks off those who pace forward with the life-force in its unhurried rhythm from those who, in the name of technical progress, hustle backwards to depletion, barrenness and exhaustion. The organic economy is accumulative. The soil itself, made out of decayed animal and vegetable matter and its bacterial agents carrying on the traffic of life, is the patient thrift of the millenniums.

The invisible bacterial world affords examples of organic power. Under favorable conditions, one bacterial cell introduced in milk can increase to number 1,024 cells in 10 hours. The human race, itself numbering uncounted millions through the ages, descended, it is believed, from one man and one woman. In our urbanized compartment we tend to think that only the machine is dynamic. But the organism represents an unhurried dynamism which in the proper environment goes forward by geometrical progression. The machine

[1] *Labor Needs to Discover Organic Power,* 1938, by G. Boyle, a pamphlet.

is depletive. It is under the law of decrease. The organism has growth and reproduction. The machine has wear and depreciation. Its depletion is not confined to itself but runs menacingly into the organic realm. Under the overwrought division of labor which is fellow-traveler of the machine we have the one-crop farmer who ships away the substance of his soil; we have the slaughtering of forests and the laying bare of the hills; we have the ripping up of sea-bottoms with trawlers and the unsettling of the environment in the delicate chain of marine life. We have, in short, a crude ignorance of natural laws.

In order properly to appreciate the good things in the technical ingenuity of man we should not disregard limitations, as is the happy faculty of, say, the advertising writer who is selling the latest thing in washing machines. The point is that we have been thinking too little of the provident dynamism of the organic powers and too much of the nihilist dynamism of the machine power. Probably, as philosophers, we haven't been any better than the advertising writer, we of the bourgeois period! After all, the wheat does not exact usury to ripen nor the corn to sprout, they cannot therefore have any funds to set aside for advertising their excellent qualities, and I mean not merely their immediate foodstuff-value but their whole existence and improvement as a phenomenon of organic power and as a fact of importance in relation to the social problem.

I say improvement, for there we have another trait of the organic thing. It is, or can be, evolutionary. By mixing of strains, animals and plants can be improved. We have many better strains of wheat today than we had in 1870. This is not to be confused with evolution of species; it has reference only to the mutability of types within the species. The change could be either up or down.

This mutability of the organic thing is, perhaps, another key to the better understanding by men of their lesser brothers—all the living. The onwardness of history seen in human events holds also in the organic. The agrarian in particular should have a sense of this procession of all the living through history, for it would help to give him respect for the organic bases of his environment. There is not only quiet power in the silent fields; there is drama and beauty. There is also harshness, horror and death. For life is a whole, and by these things is the balance kept and by enduring these does the will of man grow strong. Today, the naturalist —the man who has a philosophy of nature and the scientific insight into the plant and animal worlds—is one who will play a leading role in building a sane social order. He will be one of the key men in social education. There is a lot of refuting to be done.

The naturalist, if he has a true philosophy of nature, finds in nature the testament of the supernatural. Donald Culross Peattie describes the part insects play in the pollination of flowers and writes:

"As the dazzling spectacle of the great insect-flower symbiosis unfolded to the realization of men, wonder evoked piety. Good Pastor Sprengel used to send the fashionable congregation at Spandau away from Church without a sermon, that he might the sooner hurry into the fields. There he made brilliant observations, coloring them with a devout interpretation. . . .

"On the flowering alpine slopes of the Tyrol, Hermann Muller gave a life to the study of bees and their loves amid the flowers, and his beautiful deductions, too, pointed straight as a steeple to some divine plan nicely ordering this fraternity between the blossom and the bee."

Peattie etches, in these words, the organic foundations of even the industrialized world:

"Plant life sustains the living world; more precisely, chlorophyll does so, and where, in the vegetable kingdom, there is not chlorophyll or something closely like it, then that plant or cell is a parasite— no better, in vital economy, than a mere animal or man. Blood, bone and sinew, all flesh is grass. Grass to mutton, mutton to wool, wool to the coat on my back—it runs like one of those cumulative nursery rhymes, the wealth and diversity of our material life accumulating from the primal fact of chlorophyll's activity. The roof of my house, the snapping logs upon the hearth, the desk where I write, are my imports from the plant kingdom. But the whole of modern civilization is based upon a whirlwind spending of the plant wealth long ago and very slowly accumulated. For, fundamentally, and away back, coal and oil, gasoline and illuminating gas had green origins too. With the exception of a small amount of water power, a still smaller of wind and tidal mills, the vast machinery of our complex living is driven only by these stores of plant energy."

To the factory wage-slave conscious of hardly more than mechanized power these lines may be revealing:

"So perpetual, so terrible is the fecundity of earth that but for natural enemies any species would swiftly rise to domination, crowd itself to the point of saturation and past the point, exhaust the very chemical elements on which it lives, and die ignominiously upon the pile of its triumphs. Die of its own appalling life." [2]

Yet, everywhere are seen men swarming in thick formations about industrial centers and waging a fierce and constant struggle for wages. They have turned their backs upon the organic power. So deep had the errors of industrialism sunk into them that a few years ago the suggestion of part-time land use was looked upon with scorn. Had they not been promised a workers' paradise? Upon their dependence has been reared a certain philosophy of life—the materialistic concept of history, the class struggle, the proletariat. The removal of people from organic bases made their plight pathetic when adversity came and intensified all conditions of the conflict. Their grievance grew to become class-war and world-revolution. In 1941 the thing, twisted and confused, includes war among nations.

In comparing organic power to machine power we should not under-rate the place and importance of the latter. A swift express train, a motor car, an air-liner are magnificent creations. Who would be so foolish as

[2] *Flowering Earth,* Donald Culross Peattie. Putnam's Sons, New York, 1939, pp. 202-225, 235.

to deny technical triumphs, these the good things of technique? But the mass-surrender of living space and livelihood in order to become dependent upon the technical is another thing. This was an impulsive and irrational trend.

The extreme swing from the land has produced social convulsions. The proper order for men who would be free is, first, the organic. The organic power furnishes the conditions of liberty. The life force in the natural world about us is the covenant of the Eternal, the guarantee of basic human liberty and dignity. The failure in this industrial age, as well as the explanation of a good deal of our poverty, has been the non-recognition of this. The true order lies in the direction of an integration of the organic and the technical.

Anything else than an integration could in time bring about catastrophe. From what has already happened we get some idea of what yet could happen if the exhausting trends that go with industrialism are not changed. Centralized industry functions upon the division of labor. Division of labor, in the degree witnessed in recent decades, sets up depleting processes not only in the inorganic raw materials going into industry, but especially and more seriously in the organic resources of the regions which feed and supply the hives of industry.

This comes about by an acceptance of industrial standards in the country. A constant stream of mass-produced goods is loosed upon farmers. In order to be able to buy the farmer has to sell heavily. Home-use production is curtailed greatly by fact of the commodities and even food he and his household could produce appearing on the shelves of the local store. He becomes the blood-donor to the seller's economy. He buys more and more. He is driven to cash crop or crops. He becomes a specialist. In many cases he becomes a soil-miner or has to seek work away from the land.

To meet these standards the farmer has to sell everything he can off the place. He cannot put back into the soil what he has taken out of it. The farm tends to become a factory shipping away its substance. One-crop farming is the division of labor carried into the organic domain. Certain biologists are saying it will not work. The farm is a biological unit and must be so treated. Nature requires mixed farming. Crop rotation, animal fertilizers, proper tillage—all the ways that go with the self-sufficient family farm are right with nature.

Scientists peering into the mysteries of the world about us find sections of organic life existing as a chain. Every organism is dependent upon some other organism. An example is owls and meadow mice. If for some reason the mice of a certain area depart, the owls depart too. The same thing has been observed with fish in lakes.

If this holds in soil we get an inkling of how quick and vast can be soil depletion.

"Soil, water, air, and plant constitute a vast, intricate processing enterprise. The raw materials are humus, water, potash, nitrogen, phosphorus, lime, etc. The living beings employed in the process are the soil bacteria, earthworms, etc. There are more of these working in one square yard of good soil than there are human beings employed in the factories of a state as large as Indiana." [3]

If wheat, or cotton, or any excessive kind of one crop over-taxes a vital link in this delicately functioning creation-chamber which is soil, the structure topples. What happens is called soil erosion. The soil breaks down and is eroded or blown away. Barren sub-soil marks the passing of life. The United States loses three billion tons of good soil each year through erosion. It is stated that 59 per cent of the land surface is affected, and plant food worth $200,000,000 is lost each year.

Duncan Stewart reports in part for Canada in his book, *The Canadian Desert*. He quotes Dr. W. C. Lawdermilk as follows:

"Since May, 1934, wind erosion, set in motion by man-made forces, has transformed 5,000,000 acres of formerly good land into waste areas and great stretches of sand dunes. More than 60,000,000 acres more are in the process of wind-erosion destruction by the same cause and will follow the desert condition of the 5,000,000 destroyed acres, unless adequate control methods are undertaken."

The cutting of forests—with which to build the cities —comes in for its share of the blame. The water-containing capacity of the uplands is lowered and flood conditions come into play. The scientist tells us that it is forest cover and vegetation that control the water run-off. Run-off from unforested land is fifteen times

[3] *Rural Roads to Security*, Ligutti and Rawe. Bruce Publishing Co., Milwaukee, 1940, p. 211.

faster than from forested land. Trees, vegetation and
the attendant micro-organisms of their household constitute, as it were, an organic cap on what would be the
desert and makes possible the existence of man and
animals. Forests and the vegetal shield of earth stand
between man and extinction. An appreciative use of
the organic cap in the form of the homestead, family-
size, is the sane aim of a true sociology and also of
conservation. The depletive forces are accumulative.
Erosion becomes more dangerous as it grows. In its
early stages it is imperceptible and all the more menac-
ing for that. *Soil depletion is going on in some degree
wherever wrong methods of farming are followed.*
Break-down of soil and organic resources is a counterpart of division of labor carried out of its sphere. Is it
an exaggeration to say that the unchecked industrialism
of the tempo we've known can bring about the "abomi-
nation of desolation" which was foretold to mark the
end of the world?

New data are being obtained everywhere which
throw illumination upon the dignity and importance
of the rural callings. The farmer is the destined cus-
todian of the organic powers and of earth's flowering
heritage. Leaders in the state, awakened to the threat
of exhaustion and enfeeblement, are turning to the
home-use production-farmer with renewed acknowledg-
ments that he is the prime exemplar of citizenship. He
is as a key man, holder of a besieged line. His is a call-
ing, along with the co-operative community-building,
which will be part and parcel of the new rural movement and worthy of the best brains of the best youth
of the land.

The interdependence of the organic—from man down —must form a part of a clearer vision of our idea of the world about us. This has been swept aside by the modern preoccupation with mechanisms. The possibility of rural renewals motivated by a broad philosophical movement cannot be overlooked. Workpeople are largely determined as to the place where they shall live by economic conditions, but economic conditions are themselves the issue of the deeper thought and convictions of individuals. Economic conditions are, to a very great degree, due to a standard of values started and maintained by the few and slavishly accepted without challenge by the many. At any rate, the urban and the industrial civilization have wrought such havoc that it is necessary to marshal into the rural cause every scrap of motivation that belongs properly to it, no matter how forgotten this has been.

If the bright youths who go through the schools and colleges, that is to say who almost inevitably become urbanized, had a philosophy of nature their minds and their abilities might not be so closed against everything except the urban habitat and they could become a force in the building of the decentralist rural community. But this is yet a far cry from herding together, the surrender to bigness and to the labels of commerce which characterize the satraps of the success ideal in North America.

The sentimental outlook—as often expressed in the phrase, "back to nature"—and the betraying worship of "nature" of Rousseau have no place in the ideas making for agrarian restoration. We have to beware of the fractional mind—the type of mind which sees some fragment of truth and makes of it a whole. We are in need of nothing so much as of a rural philosophy, for urbanization seems to be an automatic process. People in the country have the right conditions for the perceptive faculties: they have some solitude. The organic tempo is favorable to assimilation, mental as well as physical. The book of nature, open the year round, cannot be put down on any printed page. But what has been lacking has been the approach. The countryman who nurtures his mind from the moods of nature is regarded as a back number. This is where the fault lies.

Every family farm that will last for generations should be stocked with literature that interprets the environment. Rural people have had very little with which to feed their minds, and most of their reading is slanted against their particular kind of life. The mind thus begins to vegetate; superstitions and half-truths take the place of knowledge. In the cityward trend the most able and ambitious have left the land; and country life, looked upon as a dying form, has not been the object of the works of the mind.

Back of rural living and under it as the foundation is that great vista—the philosophy of nature. Leaders of popular thought have not been concerned with this field in a way that influences workpeople. Its far, deep truths are needed to heal the psychological wounds of rural living. Landward progress might be helped by a new breed of scholars: the types who operate, as a bridgehead of liberty, subsistence-homesteads and therefore are not absolutely forced to adopt the views and social morals of the job-givers.

It is amazing to what a degree the economic struggle has annulled the personal views of workers. On every side people work in activities in which they do not believe, only to make a living and keep up a standard to which they are accustomed. These standards on the one hand and the insecurity on the other constitute a colossal bribery. People as dependent as are the wage-workers, with their families to look after, have ceased to be of moral significance in social reform because they have ceased to be free. Nature study has been something dismissed as a sort of fad. The lover of the birds, the open trails, fields and forest is thought to have something wrong with him. The poet is even heckled for seeing the truth:

"There was a time when meadow, grove and stream,
The earth, and every common sight,
To me did seem
Appareled in celestial light,
The glory and the freshness of a dream." [4]

The common things of land and farm are the special goods of the common man. The attitude that belittles these cuts the ground from under the common man, renders him discontented, robs him of his birthright, delivers him over as a helpless slave to materialism, and causes him to become a wanderer on the face of the earth.

A modern philosophy of nature can now be enriched by the findings from the experimental sciences. We need to try to understand the social significance of the organic powers. Above all, we need to see the whole conclave of the living in the setting of man's full destiny —the natural as the stepping-stone to the higher estates of man.

[4] Wordsworth, *Intimations of Immortality.*

CHAPTER III

Towards a Philosophy of Work

Land and the organic powers are the bases of liberty. But workpeople do not have the will to use them. Food, clothing and shelter are given to us by those basic materials and we should have the right attitude towards our materials. This attitude has been destroyed by industrialism.

A story is told of a horse that was blindfolded; he stood knee-deep in corn, but he starved to death. That horse is the figure of the chronically unemployed in North America. What has blindfolded them is industrialism and the ways of commercialism. If you look upon industry broadly as a technique of supplying people's everyday necessities you have to conclude that industry has made a poor job of it. Men starve in skills, starve in initiative, starve in foodstuffs. There are blinders on their eyes. All about them is soil-power to supply minimum wants and furnish the conditions of self-employment. From all this they are cut off by techniques of mass-production, distribution and related habits of thought.

That such a thing could happen ought to be a matter of concern in educational centers like universities which deal with the operations of the human mind. For a long time we have had a philosophy of man. But we do not hear much of a philosophy of man and his materials; that is, of a philosophy of work. For the majority, the materials are mainly land and its brood of the living.

With unemployment a chief danger-spot in society the impasse calls for a more clearly defined attitude of man towards his materials of livelihood—a philosophy of common work. This writer does not presume to be able to state such a philosophy. Anyone, however, with eyesight can see that industrialization interferes with the idea of work which men need to hold in order to be free.

Monopoly industry has separated man from his materials of living. To be cut off from supply bases and from means of self-employment not only means material insecurity but also soon creates mental disabilities. There arises what can only be termed the fractional mind: the view which sees the wage as an absolute and which holds that workers cannot do anything else but fight for wages, the view that labor is a commodity, that there are iron laws of this and iron laws of that—incomplete ideas gathered from a metallic environment.

In the dark rooms of present-day specialization a vast number of fractional minds are working, presumably in the name of science. In the name of social science men discuss current chaos as if it were merely a labor problem to be solved by the precise mathematical subtraction of so many "hands" from industry to agriculture, or vice-versa. The contingency that there may be a head and a heart connected somehow with the hands is ignored as insufferable medievalism. But from the viewpoint of a sane philosophy the social problem is more than a labor problem. The whole man is more than one of his parts, more than one of his capacities. The real problem is one of total living.

Some say that the machine age is already over. We

are entering the chemical age, they tell us. Tomorrow
the farm will be harnessed to supply the demands made
by industry as it turns to use a greater number of
organic products. That may be well or not. But even so,
life will be more than chemurgy. If it is old-fashioned
to hold that, whatever may be the current paroxysm of
progress, man still remains man, then one prefers to
be dubbed old-fashioned. What we must really be in is
some age of man—not in some fractional activity of
nature, or even of man's nature.

The proletarian is one example of the fractional man.
He is made what he is by those who gave industrialized
society its scale of values. He is the child of fractional
parents, and the agonized reaction to these fractional-
isms is the totalitarian state. The proletariat is like an
army cut off from its supply bases, an army that has
lost its maps and the reasons for its campaign. No wonder it is ready to march at the drop of the demagogue's
hat.

To hasten landward progress we must take note of all
the reasons that make common work the counterpart
of liberty.

The believer in laissez-faire told us that the machine
made as many jobs as it destroyed. But this evades two
main factors in the equation: ownership of productive
property (land), and self-employment in responsible,
creative work. Centralized industry acts against ownership and against the liberating skills and initiatives that
are the true capital of the common man. In short, what
was dangerous in the machine, used in this spirit, was
that it *gave jobs and de-humanized the worker;* for a
mere job without responsibility is sub-human. The lure

of jobs in the city drew people away from ownership of land in the country. The job ended work. The division of labor divided the man and discarded the higher part—the thinking, the responsibility.

Now there is nothing original in the view that the first law of charity is that a man take care of himself when able. As long as he does not infringe upon the rights of others, this has always been recognized as valid. By taking care of himself he relieves others of the need of doing it. It follows that the large degree of self-sufficiency of which the productive rural home is capable (when rescued from the inefficiencies of commercialism) represents high moral and social value. The most menial work reaches a high plane—it reaches the degree and worth and nobility that is in inverse proportion to the breakdown and agony in society. The more contentious and despairing industrial conditions become, the more obviously the saving qualities of the farm-craft community shine out by comparison.

This first law of charity is also the first law of social reform. If you rehabilitate the family through land and crafts, society is in that much better position to take care of itself. An Agrarian Movement could legitimately become conscious of itself as the true social-reform movement. Subsistence-farming should take on the importance hitherto taken on by reformers who found in the social unrest an opening for careers. This social consciousness is, of itself, another factor to be used to remake the pride and self-respect of rural living. Farming should now be brought out as a social profession. And it is not too much to ask that the professional reformers and the careerists of confusion be expected to exemplify their social ideals in promoting the decentralist community.

I do not know whether or not the sane leaders of our day can give to the tiller-owner (not to the commercial farmer who follows the errors of industrialism) what the Marxist leaders gave to the proletariat. Can they give him the consciousness of a world mission, one for a man to achieve not by scaling the great altitudes of economic and political regimentation but within the confines of his own line-fences? This tiller class is the class with obvious historical meaning. Its value has never been stated—at least not in the trumpeted and compelling tones of its rivals. And the reason is that the intellectuals have become a part of the entourage of urbanism. The seller's culture has swallowed the human mind.

This social outlook will be proper to the new rural communities—co-operative settlements more compact than the old, settlements that through use of soil can integrate the organic forces with a human scale technology. This social outlook would be one of the dynamics in their philosophy of work.

But a philosophy of work concerns most closely the person. The wage-system acted against a true idea of work, and it is among the victims of industrialization that the fractional concept of work is held. With the rise of the wage-system men sold labor. The sub-human waiting-for-a-job mentality set in. Smart men went far in good jobs. But the broad mass of common men (the chief concern of society) fared badly. The development of skills awaited the wage job. If the job didn't come, the young worker became a tramp. In many cases the job took less and less skill. We are all familiar with the type of unemployed who is now unemployable. The man who waited for a wage job to develop, himself may never be developed, for he may never get the job and even if he does it may not last. By these steps fifty-year-old men become vagrants.

The artist—and every man is potentially an artist—knows that the capacity to work well is first of all a big spiritual investment. The will-to-work should never be foiled by so fickle and confining a thing as a job. A man must even be willing to work for no wage rather than forego the dowry of the workman—the initiative, skills, vision, patience, concentration, judgment, perseverance, hardiness, power to plan, love of materials—as the woodsman loves a tree—and joy in execution.

People who wait for jobs do not develop these psychological equipments. Thereby hangs the tale of the million marching feet of the unemployment army. In that army we see industrialism's lethal toll upon the human personality. For land and home-crafts provide the materials of work for people of the humblest talents. The right of men to work and through work to receive this endowment of qualities is prior to the paltry ritual of subjection to that particular standard of living which arises from the financier's desire to sell mass-produced goods. The tragedy is that if people held onto this philosophy of provident work they would be in a better position to enjoy some of the technical good things too.

Work is human; it is necessary to man for two reasons: to provide and to express. Both provision and expression are necessary to be human. To be provided for is not, of itself, enough. To give expression (that is, to place the imprint of the personality upon materials) , to develop one's brain, skill and will is not, of itself, enough. Both must be realized.

Throughout history prior to industrialism there was usually plenty of work to be done. But often scanty provision. It remained for industrialism, in the name of progress, to destroy both provision and expression for considerable numbers of people. It did this because the seller's culture fostered vogues that divorced populations from their bases of livelihood. It persuaded them not to make the things they could make. It created the over-serviced generation—the jobless. Instalment buying is one example of an activity based upon the dissolution of a philosophy of work; it is founded upon the imbecile premise that not only can you eat your cake and have it, but that you should even eat it before you've earned it. To break the dark misery-making of this kind of thing will be a great step towards progress and towards the liberation of the human spirit from the witchcraft of modern commercialism.

Before we can get anywhere in a land movement we must re-establish a scale of values in work. In the creative order the farmer and the craftsman do work that is superior to that of the traders. A truly human order would never permit trade to dominate. We have had no philosophy of work; we have had a philosophy of evading work. The well-to-do amass profits so as to be able to get rid of work. They take from the many the work which the many need to do in order to live. The unlimited-profit motive destroyed work. Work gets done up ahead. The drive for profits brings over-production. The getting of fortunes by the fortunate and the standards they set make the poor ashamed to engage in what they consider to be menial work. Farming is considered to be in this category.

Of old it was said: "Thy work is thy portion." It is by work that the abilities to plan, design, execute are exercised. These abilities make man human. (Only the animal is mere consumer, and not all animals at that.) Out of these abilities are derived the inner satisfactions which make for wholesome and hearty living. If you take away these satisfactions of man's creative bent you leave a psychic hiatus. Behold the frustrated and floundering individual! Work-need is much more than bread-need. Work is the spindle upon which are spun the threads of a man's life. The man who really idles is always hurting himself.

Governments have had to spend large sums on "agricultural relief." In the state of frustration to which the farmer has been reduced this has to be done—for a time. But there is something extremely unwholesome about the whole business of people trained by the system to non-use of the materials of livelihood all around them. It confirms the view that the genuine thing to do is to teach the people a philosophy of work. That includes a diagnosis which reveals the agencies that act against home-production of necessities; it includes also the building of a mind resistant to such agencies.

Commercialism has demonstrated that people today are completely helpless regarding economic custom and choice of commodities. They put aside genuine homemade things for inferior "boughten" things. They trade themselves into insolvency and think it progress—under the spell of advertising. But the point to be noted here

is that they are susceptible to argument. Men who are
leaders—who have enough influence to set styles and
vogues—can turn the tide. We need propaganda—mighty
like a tempest—setting forth the good points of home-
use production, teaching a philosophy of work as the
master-concept of a true agrarianism.

It is much better that this be done by private agencies
than by the state. Is it so remarkable that education
has not defended the hearths of the people better? Con-
ventional education is most accurately characterized
as absent-minded. In an agrarian restoration adult education will find a glorious piece of work. To reunite
man with land without putting aside the rational use
of the technical good things is a real challenge.

The commonest work is of such value to the human
soul that it would be impossible to over-romanticize or
over-dramatize work. In the Christian idea of work,
the more lowly the work the greater the merit in at
least one respect, as lowly work is a high form of
humility. Christianity taught men to be at once proud
and humble. It is well to remember this, for a man
should be proud of his work even if it be only the
making of an ax-handle.

Pride in common work as well as humility are not
possible without meditation: a philosophy of work
leads into the very depths of the spirit. The criticism
that is often leveled at rural life is that it is monotonous.
The farm youth sees the dapper roadster swishing by
and feels that his work is by comparison dull and
monotonous. He is mistaken even here. The man in
the roadster soon finds it more monotonous than the
youth finds the field. The field is a theater of constantly

changing life. Peattie, the naturalist, has recorded the wonder and ecstasy of great men when they turned the "lens on the face of nature." The farmer walks amid mystery and finds it dull until his eyes are opened to it.

As a matter of fact some monotony is an importation from mechanical work where there is no mental exertion and conquest. Monotony belongs to work which one does not love. Repetition goes with common work, but repetition is not necessarily monotonous. Routine may be due, not to lack of life, but to a rush of life, Chesterton knew. He wrote:

> "The thing I mean can be seen, for instance, in children, when they find some game or joke that they specially enjoy. A child kicks his legs rhythmically through excess, not absence of life. Because children have abounding vitality, because they are in spirit fierce and free, therefore they want things repeated and unchanged. They always say, 'do it again'; and the grown-up person does it again until he is nearly dead. For grown-up people are not strong enough to exult in monotony. But perhaps God is strong enough to exult in monotony. It is possible that God says every morning, 'Do it again' to the sun; and every evening, 'Do it again' to the moon." [1]

Monotony has been pinned on rural work by anti-rural propagandists whose eyes were closed to nature's endless designing. But monotony belongs to the field of the automata, not to the field of organisms. In the onwardness of life there is always drama—if we know

[1] *Orthodoxy,* G. K. Chesterton. Dodd, Mead & Co., New York, 1927, pp. 92, 93.

how to look. Monotony, mechanism, materialism is the urban trinity of death. The vast entertainment-business of the modern city is invented for the chief purpose of rescuing people from the monotony of their work and environment. It is the visitor who finds the country monotonous, not the farmer. The farmer is too near the purposes of life to evaluate them so wrongly.

Msgr. Fulton Sheen is close to some of Chesterton's thought when he writes:

"There is necessarily bound to be a thrill in working toward any goal or fixed purpose, and therein is the final reason for the romance of repetition. There, too, is the line of division between genuine Christianity and modern paganism. The Christian finds a thrill in repetition because he has a fixed goal; the modern pagan finds repetition monotonous because he has never decided for himself the purpose of living. Instead of passing the test, the modern mind changes the test; instead of working toward an ideal, it changed the ideal; instead of tending repetitiously toward a fixed point, the modern mind changed its point of view, and calls it progress. It is no wonder life is dull, when one has not decided on what the purpose of life is; it is no marvel that existence is drab, if one has never discussed the reason for existence." [2]

Wage-work for the great majority of common workers is merely for the wage. There is no love of the work, but only of the money—which the system has taught the worker to need so badly. Nothing would be

[2] *Moods and Truths*, Fulton J. Sheen. D. Appleton-Century Co., New York.

more futile than to try to put people on land if they still have the wage-mentality. There is such a thing as good housekeeping and good husbandry, but farming cannot be reduced to business. It has too much of the immeasurable in it—the immeasurable that belongs not to materials but to the spirit that is in things that live. To figure the immediate cash return for work is the fatal folly of the squatter, on land today, on relief tomorrow.

The farmer, who has a philosophy of work, builds soil, follows nature's laws, is not awed by unnatural wants; thinking in terms of generations he builds an organic estate.

A spirit of work is impossible without meditation. It is impossible without a literature, which today does not exist in the rural community, a literature that sees in and around the personal and the social reflexes of work and how it strikes into the heart of things. Monotony belongs to the jaded materialism of our age which, busied with industrialism, has lost the sense of drama in Creation. Contemplation gives tone to work. Work is engrossing only when its effects inside and upon the outer world are projected upon the mind. The hill of potatoes planted, the floor scrubbed clean fit clearly into the picture of man's care and are swept up into the dignity which belongs to mankind's suffering and ascent to God. The workman, the artisan who loves his work, knows his little part in the drama of life. If his part is small he knows that the play is a great one. Like an actor he goes out on the stage to say his lines and to do his part with gusto.

Work that is fully human is not all drudgery and it is

not all joy. It is a mosaic of the main strands of existence. It is never free from exertion, either mental or
physical, and out of effort comes its satisfying power.
It is the chief exerciser of the worker's will. To provide,
to express, to contemplate, to will and to do it daily—
that is work.

The flight, on the part of the poor man, from self-
employment on the land probably is the same in motive
as the greed of the fortune-hunter. Both seek to im-
munize themselves from work. It is said by some that
work is for the sake of leisure as war is for the sake of
peace. But work has value in itself apart from leisure.
This is shown by the fact that people who have leisure
have to invent work to do.

Medical science, especially the branch having to do
with mental states, recognizes the curative power of
work. Likewise moral science. Gabriel Francis Powers,
in the book *Redemption* (Good Shepherd Press,
Manila), describes how fallen women and girls, broken
in spirit, are rehabilitated with best results by working
on land. This is quite understandable. The multiplied
tensions of the world-city places intolerable strains
upon sensitive natures. At the opposite end of the scale
the author of *We Farm for a Hobby and Make It Pay*
shows how children develop in character and self-
reliance through the disciplines and creative activities
of farm life. A city child is seldom called on to exercise
initiative or accept responsibility; a child on a farm
must handle animals, remember feeding and milking
times, fasten gates, turn off faucets, observe unusual
happenings and report them with the possibility of real
loss and harm ensuing should he fail to do so. Nature on

a farm educates the child in ways that in a city can be replaced only artificially and very inadequately. Making children active, a farm life makes them happy.

In idleness, life loses all meaning. That is the problem for those who proclaim this to be the age of plenty and of leisure. Work is zestful in accordance with how greatly it is needed by ourselves or others. A finished world, that is a workless world, would indeed be monotonous. Employment in mechanized industry, with the exception of the comparatively few planners, does not measure up to that fullness of functioning which is human work. It cannot be a maker of the full human being. The worker may become a full human being by his extra-work activities, but it is in spite of his work and not by help of it.

A philosophy of work will include the right use of leisure. Many people recoil from farm life because on the homestead endless work stares one in the face. That is true. But can it be ignored that the influx of commercial products to the rural home keeps the farmer's nose to the grindstone to meet the bills? He has fired at him a town culture to be grafted on a rural base. That culture enslaves him, causes him to fail. He becomes bitter and leaves the land. This subject will be touched on in a later chapter. Let it also be noted that a rural *culture* has never been undertaken in North America. When we got the land cleared and the houses built we began to move cityward; we adopted a town culture; the two do not mix at all points. Rural life has been stagnant first, then in retreat. Argument for rural life in these pages is not argument for the rural *status quo*.

To work properly, leisure is needed. To enjoy leisure there must be security. The job-holder who may be fired next month cannot know the meaning of leisure. On the properly conceived farmstead the conditions of leisure are present, for nature in her unfolding of the seasons and in the organic tempo of seeding, growth, harvest has left many spaces which fit the psychic states of man. The rural environment furnishes the conditions for the working-out of a philosophy of work and the building of an indigenous culture. Had we consciously worked at and taught these, the uprooting of populations that is taking place on this continent might not have happened.

Capitalist economics with a certain quack realism shoved aside one of the greatest motive powers of mankind. It is what Ruskin refers to as the affective side of economics: the worker works best with what he loves. The idea that the most is gotten out of workmen by the competitive wage-system Ruskin refutes in these words:

"It would be so if the servant were an engine of which the motive power was steam, magnetism, gravitation, or any other agent of calculable force. But he being, on the contrary, an engine whose motive power is a Soul, the force of this very peculiar agent, as an unknown quantity, enters into all the political economist's equations, without his knowledge, and falsifies every one of their results. The largest quantity of work will not be done by this curious engine for pay, or under pressure, or by help of any kind of fuel which may be applied by the chaldron. It will be done only when the motive force, that is to say, the will or spirit of the creature, is brought to its greatest strength by its own proper fuel; namely by the affections." [3]

In rural work the affections enter to a special degree. We know of the brotherhood of man. There is also that other great brotherhood of all the living of which the farm is the home. A man may love his horses, his herds and his sheep and the proud flock that struts in the poultry yard; he may love the trees, the bearing orchard, the field and the plants; he may find that work in this environment is much more than barren toil.

What a true philosophy of work would mean to the home life of the mainly self-sufficient farm household is beyond the saying. It would be the light of the home and its armory. Home under the wage way of life becomes a jumping-off station, a place where things are merely consumed and as a consequence a nucleus of boredom.

It is the people who try to run farms as businesses that go bankrupt. They also destroy the organic cap. Who is there that has not been intrigued by the thought that it is our richest regions in soil, where monoculture for cash is dominant, that have advancing tenantry? It is in the rich valleys that you will find the big mortgage figures and the dying ownership. But up on the hillsides, you will still find, here and there, the diversifying farmer and craftsman; very often he finishes his days with title to the property unsmirched and with a bank account.

[3] *Unto This Last,* John Ruskin. Ginn & Company, Boston, 1894, p. 119.

Nature takes strange revenges upon those who would pin her down to mathematics. She provisions him who knows her law and works in conformity with it, but her bookkeeping she reveals to no man. For mystery and suspense and faith are the main foods of our life, and the explained no longer draws us on.

CHAPTER IV

Common Work and Culture

"The farther we get away from the rough work of the farm the more we are able to devote ourselves to cultural pursuits."

There are few people who have not heard the foregoing idea expressed in some form or other. Our schools and universities, our literature and our drama, our salesmanship and our connoisseurs of leisure have been saying it in ten thousand ways. The proposition is fairly representative of the outlook of our time.

In this proposition, as expressed above, we in North America are affirming something more than a conviction; we are telling something of our history. We are saying, in effect, that we never seriously considered making a rural culture. Whether we thought about it or not we have acted in such a way that now to a great many people land and culture are incompatible. This is largely responsible for the drained-away condition of population in the rural communities.

Culture has been thought of as an urban something.[1] There is such a thing as an urban culture. It is not the purpose of these chapters to evaluate it. But has

[1] Spengler wrote that, "All great Cultures are town-Cultures." *Vis-à-vis* Spengler's line of prediction, Eric Gill's view that a culture should be based upon necessary work is most revolutionary.

What Spengler wrote is true in the sense that it has been in the towns that cultures flower, wither and die. But town culture is fed from the country. Rural life and the genius of place nurse and strengthen the specific traits in human character. These in the mixture are the creative elements upon which urban cultures are maintained.

not the assumption been quite prevalent that urban culture is the only culture worth the name? It is obvious that this narrows and emasculates the idea of culture. Order is a true requisite of liberty. And, applied to material things, variety belongs to the concept of order. It is the arrangement of different notes that make harmony. A monoculture is tyrannical. It is monotonous and sterilizing.

The idea of culture is an exceedingly complicated one. It is the mosaic of all the beliefs and works of a people. A people without positive beliefs cannot have a full culture; and there are valid distinctions between culture and civilization. In fact, in certain modern senses of the word "civilized" the two are opposed.[2]

I think one of the most harmful assumptions that we have around us is that culture is something necessarily foreign to the rural community. The pride of the cities is a kernel in our brand of culture. The best educated youth become urbanized. If not, they are hardly thought to be a success. Now, here is where a curious anomaly comes in. The urbanizing process is demonstrably hurting the nation and, in the long reckonings of population growths, urbanization is suicide. Fixedness in style and in the mere formats of living enfeebles the soul. Hence we find as one of the dominants in our bogus culture something that is indistinguishable from pride in self-extinction. Somewhere between this and the very isolated type of rural living there must be a middle way.

It is sad to see how widely this view is held. Culture,

[2] See Herbert Agar's book *Land of the Free.* Houghton Mifflin Co., Boston, 1935.

it seems, has come to be understood as merely polish. Our country people have the idea that culture is something apart from common work. Thus the great dimensions of beauty, of zest, of pride, are taken from work and it becomes dull and is drudgery.

I once had a talk with a man who was doing educational work in a village. I told him I thought that if the young people were not to be attracted from farms into the towns they would have to be given a sense of culture in the villages. He suspected me at once of being high-hat. The word culture "got" him. He seemed to think that I was proposing that the farmers should be "citified." No doubt he imagined how absurd it would be to consider the farmer doing the barn-work with a white collar and brightly polished shoes. Culture seemed to be apart from this sturdy life. One gets the same reaction if one mentions culture—without explanation—at rural gatherings. The audience is apt to look up with an expression that says:

"He can't mean us. It's high-brow. All right for New York, Toronto, or some such place. But it doesn't belong here. Here, we work for a living!"

This same attitude is representative of rural life in most places. It is typical of the low estimate the rural mind has come to have of its own works and environment. It is a false and deadly view, an ally of discontent and of the trend cityward. So deep has struck the heresy that an authentic culture can only be of the urban brand!

It is arguable whether or not polish is an ingredient of any importance in culture. St. Paul described himself as crude in speech, but not in knowledge. Yet it was that Jew, wrote Maritain, who carried all Europe in his arms. This much seems certain: the cultured man would not be too polished; he would believe some things to be of such importance that he might do violence to you if you menaced them. All through history it has been some fierce believer who threw over idols and dashed aside the shibboleths of effete followers of the vogue.

In most parts of our continent people who stayed on the land took the view, implicit in the attitude of the educated, and suggested in the opening paragraph of this chapter. The spurious idea of culture, that it consists in various external trivia and saponaceous manners and especially in the conspicuous consumption of the latest nationally advertised goods, has been accepted and unquestioned as culture. As a consequence we have people living dejectedly on the land and anxious to get out of their implied cultural inferiority at the first opportunity.

This attitude is traceable to the commonly accepted view that to be cultured you should be able to live on the labor that other people do; that, in short, you should be a fancier of the work, art and creations of others rather than be a workman yourself.

I do not think that there is hope for an agrarian restoration without a change in this idea of culture. People do not do work well in which they have no heart. Pride in work and self-respect are the psychological substances that must enter into a renewed rurality. Unless the convictions that will let people live on the land with pride and spirit can be uncovered and dramatized, we may as well reconcile ourselves to their becoming the dole-wards of the state.

Agrarians should not underestimate the strength of the forces against them. The lure of the bright lights is a very strong one. What we are up against is described by Jacob E. Lange, of Odense, Denmark:

> "When in a murky night the lonely farmer stands outside his home he may discern in one direction or another a slight illumination of the sky near the horizon. And he knows then that this is the reflection of the lights of a distant town, and instinctively it attracts him as the flame attracts the moth.
>
> "It is not merely the cinema, the glaring illuminated streets, etc., that draw the country population to the cities. Far more the attraction springs from a feeling of desolation and dreariness as compared with what looks like a higher, brighter existence, a life of richer, more enlightened activity, a more really human world. Under the influence of this state of mind the rural populations dwindle, even in the most fertile agrarian states.
>
> "The farmer's wife on the solitary prairie farm dreams of a town life without her daily routine of tedious work, a kitchen with running water, hot and cold, next at hand an electric stove and superior schooling for her growing-up children. The schoolmistress in the lonely one-room schoolhouse is constantly looking forward from Monday to Friday for her weekend trip in her little car to town, dreaming dreams of a preferment that will take her to an urban community, be it ever so small. To live on Main

Street to her is high life compared to her life on a dirt road far away. No wonder that her pupils will think and dream the same dream and turn their back to the farm whenever possible.

"And the lonely farmer dreams and conjectures in a similar way, swept away by the same current. Land speculation does the rest. In boom times farmers will sell their land at an exorbitant price and go to town to live in a villa as independent gentlemen, and their successors, burdened with exorbitant mortgages, often struggle in vain against adversity and in hard times go broke and likewise drift into town, to swell the tide of the unemployed." [3]

Although boom times for farmers seem gone forever there is always to be noted this trend: as soon as the farmer becomes well-to-do he is likely to leave the land and move to town. In the middle western states, in the wheat belt of western Canada, in Prince Edward Island, in the Annapolis Valley of Nova Scotia—wherever you find rich farmlands—you will find towns made up of farmers who made enough money to move in and go into business.

It would seem that as the economic condition of rural people improves they tend to leave the land. And the conclusion is inescapable that a balance of populations can only be kept by a consciously defined and emphasized culture. This would mean a change in the direction of the village form of rural life and away from the layout of lonely farms far separated in the open country. A culture implies numbers.

[3] *Rural America*, March, 1940.

A short time ago I heard college students debate whether or not unemployment could be lowered by putting people on the land. One side argued that rural resettlement was not feasible because more attractive conditions of living in towns and cities would sooner or later draw people off the land. That this tendency exists was not only not denied, rather it was established as the very reason why it is now so necessary to proclaim a rural philosophy and to seek out the basis of a proud rural culture. The slide cityward is automatic. And the clogged city means decay of men. Ultimately the politics of this top-heavy centralism is the tyrant state.

In short we must either busy ourselves with reaffirming and building the bases of a rural culture or be prepared to submit to accumulative urbanization and all its dire consequences. Some will argue that this can only come with the stark, drastic discipline and effective delusions which go with dictatorship. But on this great unfilled continent we stand on Freedom. It seems to be the mission of free men to work towards a free solution in nations where the theory of freedom is still held in respect.

The well-to-do tend to leave the land and follow the excitements of city life. Hence the question arises: Why use the economic approach—as adult educators in Nova Scotia have been doing in seeking to improve the lot of farmers and fishermen? Why talk about the price of fish and fertilizer? Why build co-operative stores and credit unions when at bottom the problem is one of making a rural culture?

The answer is twofold. First, the economic is necessary in a culture—it is like the iron that is a necessary nucleus in the human blood cell. Second, there is the question of a means. If a rural and provident culture is the thing for very considerable numbers of people, there must be evolved the agencies of enlightenment to teach it, to defend it, and to implement it. Otherwise we would have merely a fine idea, a disembodied abstraction which very few could follow, and no fecundity. We must evolve our sinews of war as we go along: the tremendous significance of credit unions and co-operatives cannot be overestimated in the new agrarianism. In this sense the economic end necessarily comes in as an essential. But a man's economic conduct is something that arises out of his moral and psychological states. And no reform can be worth much or be lasting unless it reaches these moral levels.

The rise of laissez-faire, of economic liberalism and of mass-production, was not only an economic change; it was at root a moral sundering of which the advent of the machine was the occasion. The apologists of the perversion were hard pushed for a long time to justify it. To do so they had to set up a contradiction which was to pull the common man at once in two directions. Liberalism made the possession of material goods the norm, the great desire, the chief end, and then let loose the frenzy of unbridled competition that made it impossible for great numbers of the poor and the working classes to obtain the goods or even to get enough to eat. This contradiction at the heart of economic liberalism accounts for the frustration and bitterness that leads to revolution. Liberalism set up a goal, emblazoned it, and made the achievement of it by the masses impossible. Not only that, but the condition by which the fortunate few reached the goal was that a whole host of others should never be able to reach it, yet must ever have it dangled in front of them. The money-lenders wax strongest on the economics of scarcity.

As a result we have inherited today in secular culture a deadly set of standards. The poor, and the burden comes hardest on the young, are bludgeoned with a material standard of living which they cannot meet. It all bears some resemblance to the spectacle of the martyrs of old who were pulled apart alive by having their limbs hitched to horses moving in opposite directions. One has only to recall the hopeful and haggard line-up at any employment agency of a large city even in the prosperous middle twenties to understand the wrenching of the heart and the twisting of the dagger. We witness today some changing of these norms. In several nations service to the state has become the success ideal.

Before there can be an effective decentralist movement and a rural revival, forgotten sets of values will have to be uncovered and affirmed in a way sufficiently moving to cause men of ability to go and live the life. It seems to me that it is with one of these forgotten values that Eric Gill dealt in a lecture before the Royal Society of Arts, London, April, 1938.

"The object of this lecture is to support the thesis that human culture is the product of necessary work and not, as is commonly supposed and often stated, the product of leisure—meaning by leisure not those conditions of working in which a contemplative or deliberative state of mind is possible, but simply the

time during which men are not earning their livings
by doing work for which they are paid." [4]

The idea of necessary work as a base of culture is one
that offers possibilities in the revival of a rural spirit.
If we look into the history of the divorcement of people
from common work we shall find that they were persuaded that their work was both unnecessary and uncul-
tural. That is how they came to be over-serviced,
de-skilled and workless. This seduction goes on progressively. Why, it goes under the very name of Progress!
What else is the appeal of, for instance, the radio salesman? His honeyed tones suggest to the housewife that
it is utterly unnecessary for her to make her own cheese
or jam or canned foods when the prepared imitation
is upon every counter. Really nice people do not do
this any more, it is implied by radio-voice, by vogue,
by a million glittering and anti-social lies in the ad
pages of the slick papers and magazines. Anti-social, I
say, because they destroy work-qualities in people and,
within a generation or two, leave them spiritless, en-
feebled, jobless, homeless, and wards of some kind of
dictator.

Rod MacSween, agricultural representative, Antigonish, Nova Scotia, has told me of the folklore that was
current in the days when pioneers were conquering the
forests of this continent. What he was talking about
were the settlements of Highland Scots in Cape Breton
Island, Nova Scotia. Within a generation or two these
pioneers had built fairly self-sufficient communities.

[4] Published under the title of *Work and Culture,* by John Stevens,
29 James St., Newport, Rhode Island, 1938.

When men gathered at the neighbor's house in the evening they would talk of their work. While the young listened, those talkers really formed a sort of informal discussion circle. The fathers talked about the deeds of work: of chopping down forests, of clearing and breaking land, of building houses and barns, of planting and harvest and husbandry. And on these talks were woven, unconsciously perhaps, the traits that make good citizens—the will-to-work, valor and skill, patience and foresight. Those men were dramatizing necessary work. Without thinking of it, they were teaching attitudes needed for independent living suited to their time. They were teaching a profound social philosophy. With such a strand kept strong in the culture great inequalities due to poverty were at a minimum.

Within the last year Dr. Sexton of the Nova Scotia Technical College gave a report on unemployed young men in what are now industrial towns in this same region. The striking thing, of course, was the dearth of opportunity for young men. The report stated:

"None of them had been employed for any considerable proportion of the time since they had left school. A few had never had more than a pick-and-shovel job for a week or two on relief projects in a period of three or four years. Some men of 24 and 25 had not had enough time at work to total six months altogether in the seven or eight years that they had been seeking employment. Only three or four per cent had been able to get any experience that could be called skilled. About one-fifth to one-quarter of the young men had never worked at all for wages.

None of them had been able to get a foothold from which they could proceed to learn a skilled trade or to obtain any degree of security in employment."

Back of the home-crafts is the sound base of a folk-culture. It only awaits popularization and the toning down of the seller's culture, its opposite—which would put into the hands of rural people about everything ready-made.

Hence the agrarian community of the future cannot conceive of itself as a community in retreat, with a squalid destiny below the cultural line, but on the contrary should take the initiative, conscious that land, crafts and Co-operation are bases of a provident culture. In short, we go to the land in the name of culture and not in renunciation of it.

Eric Gill makes several distinctions in the meaning of culture. Culture, he says, is cultivation according to nature. The most inclusive and fundamental cultivation is religious cultivation. It pierces all others. Man needs cultivation with a view to the after-life. But there are also the more particular ends of their life. On this ground culture becomes diversified—or rather it should, in spite of monopoly capitalism which tried to make us believe that culture was acceptance of the goods and standards which secured its money profit.

"Thus the culture of a peasantry is different from that of a factory town.

"The culture of a class of persons living on dividends is different from that of people who earn their livings.

"And to come down to individuals, the culture of a blacksmith is different from that of a clerk." [5]

I think most persons can agree with Mr. Gill. On this concrete ground you cannot, with any meaning, speak of culture as an abstract thing, for there are only different cultures. And the culture derives from the kind of work the person does. As a great variety of work is needed with which citizens can supply themselves and the needs of society, it is evident that the essential note in culture on this plane is that it be multiform and varied. It is here that variation in nature delivers men from the death-leveling of standardization. (All dead men behave alike.)

There are levels of culture which rightly involve certain uniformities such as the religious culture, the national and the racial culture. But the culture that derives from work is the product, rich in variety, of the human personality confronting its environment. This work-day arena of mind and spirit and body is the principal ground of life's experience for the average man. That it has not been presented to him as being truly cultural, was due to the fact that agencies which wanted to do his work for a profit were influential enough to liquidate a full and true concept of culture.

I can best illustrate what I mean by an example. Let us consider a case quite common in land settlement. We shall call this family the Russells. Henry Russell, his wife and five children have been struggling to build a home on the land. He started with very little in 1932 and today has a respectable house, seventy acres of land,

[5] *Work and Culture*, Eric Gill, 1938.

of which eighteen acres are in fair cultivation. He manages to feed and clothe his family but not much more. In these nine years there have been times when there was not enough clothing or proper food. Russell is something of an artisan and so is his wife. There are also a few skilled workmen in the neighborhood. It would be easy for them to furnish their house almost completely out of materials on the place. They could thus save some hundreds of dollars, besides getting some fun out of designing and having about them ideas of their own embodied in art. But they will not do this. The reason is that the articles thus produced do not measure up to the fashion dictates of the day. The more uppish friends of the family would not be impressed. In the community there are not even available models from which good style furniture could be made.

Let us take an opposite case. Recently I accompanied A. B. MacDonald on a trip to a part of Nova Scotia, he being on his way to organize the 196th credit union in the Province. At a certain place we stopped before a cluster of overnight cabins. Modern of moderns is the overnight cabin, and these looked just right from the outside. Mr. MacDonald engaged one for the night. To our surprise we found, when we got inside, that the cabins were outfitted in handicraft. The interior was redolent of the woodworker's shop. Native wood spiced the air. Bedsteads, chairs, bureaus, window sashes and fixtures were all made from seasoned wood, all looking as though they had their origins on the timbered hillside 300 yards behind the cabins. They were made in fitting style. They exemplified simple craft at its best and were the epitome of localism. They were *sui generis.* Something of the spirit of that locality seemed to be in this simple furniture.

The traveler was glad to pay $1.50 to spend the night there. Here, we reflected, the things that rural people had somehow come to reject were being popularized commercially. There is something ironic about it all. As we looked around this charming cabin so spic and span with the pungent odor of planed wood and the natural colors, we could not but think of bedrooms we had seen so often in rural homes. A meager ensemble of mass-produced stuff! In most rural houses you might see anything except the handmade article because the people had been brought to the point where they think that handicraft is disgraceful. They would have plenty of timber on the place to furnish those rooms, there would be potential craftsmen in the neighborhood who would make a good job of it; yet it would not be done, for it was not the style. It would not add anything to the profits of the big furniture makers, so it was not the style.

Advertising, the mail-order catalogue, the magazine pages, the subtle-tongued vanities propagated by salesmanship have done their work well. The wife of Farmer Russell will not stand for the homecraft stuff. Now, if the Russells could furnish their bedrooms with the high-priced furnishings no one would object. The mere killing of local craftsmanship as an art is an accident which industrialism is capable of ignoring. But many of the Russells—millions of the Russells—cannot do this. So the Russells begin to feel the pinch. They become disgruntled, discouraged in the course of time, for this applies not merely to furnishing a bedroom or two, or even a house, but to several other departments of the Home-on-the-Land. Presently the Russells pull out. The nearest town or city receives the hopeful family. The fate of man is to be where creative work is. If creative work is decentralized, people are decentralized. "Thy work is thy portion." The further steps in the destroying of the Russell family are familiar. Unemployment, relief, social break-down are terminal stages of the ordeal.

Thus has the witchcraft of commercialism displaced the true crafts of people and destroyed the sense of culture and true art, which if defended and kept up from generation to generation would strengthen self-employing populations on the land. Is it any use denying that the class of unemployed which our labor departments consider unemployable are the creations of this commercialism? The unemployable are in a basic sense uncultured. Yet they have been made this way in the name of pseudo-culture.

I think that the great irony of the social crisis in North America is that it has been caused by gentlefolk who love their kittens. They wouldn't hurt a fly. They only gave the emphasis of their lives to the dramatization of superficial and uprooting values. In a way the thing would be more tolerable if it had been performed by frank tyrants and their ax-men in the name of destiny. Then it could be fought. But these people who love their dogs and give alms to the poor, yet give their lives to the propagation of the betraying standards are not bloodthirsty. They are only blind. In their absent-minded way they suck the blood of infants.

It seems to me the question before social education

is this: can the moral and intellectual forces be moved to sponsor rural life as a culture, not merely as a place to go when somebody gets broke? It should be the mission of whatever leadership we have to give rural life the consciousness of itself as a base of culture so that plain men will be permitted again to provision themselves from their own land with pride. This will take something much more than sounding off resolutions in favor of rural life at conventions. It will certainly involve in many quarters, if it is done at all, a re-examination of what we have been assuming to be culture. We shall have to find men and women of ability and vigor to champion the life and to go and live it.

If terrible tempests have descended upon the democracies we have to remember that the meanest of historical falsifications of culture is that which would take from the common man his self-respect in doing the work necessary to keep himself from being a slave. You thus take the heart out of him. In raising the banner of a culture based on necessary work it is not well to oversimplify. Something very vital can be revived in the heart of the ordinary individual who finds new cause and dignity in daily endeavor. But there are, of course, wider fields. Necessary work is a wide category; it includes not only use of land and the provident crafts but also the tapping of the people's heritage through the building of co-operatives.

CHAPTER V

Land versus Totalitarianism

Wɪᴛʜ the advance of industrialism came the decline of rural life and the growth of uprooted populations in the cities. People had turned from the organic bases of soil to the technical bases of machinery; what was personal and responsible in work was progressively eliminated. Ownership of land that would provide for a man and his family had vastly declined. By the time the Great Depression was seven years old many realized that civilization was out on a limb. But just how far out was not realized until in 1939 the War broke out. Then the world slowly awakened to the fact that Nazi Germany had forged socialized industry into a sword. As a result, there is danger that other nations may be drawn into a state of tribal collectivism with a Chief.

Industry for profit had been the cry of the capitalist. Industry for service had been the cry of the Christian and the Socialist. Now come the frank tyrants with the cry, industry for domination. The world suddenly begins to realize what price it may have to pay for its overstressing of the "soulless competence of the merely technical." Industry operated in accordance with the "love principle," as Kagawa calls Co-operation, would be Christian. Industry for conquest is worse than pagan.

The industrial system, according to Nazi thinking, is the means not of progress but of domination. Machine dynamism—the drive that is in the machine—has awaited a ruthless enough hand to reveal this, its true character. Hermann Rauschning makes this clear in a book he wrote in 1937-38.[1] Rauschning had been a member of the Nazi Party and cannot be accused of any anti-German bias.

In the Nazi outlook the theories of Marx and Bismarck are merged and come of age. Marx closed his eyes to a great world-class of owners of means of production and potential exemplars of production for use—the farmers—and built his plans of revolution squarely upon the wage proletariat. He, too, considered surrender to the technical trend irresistible. He referred to the idiocy of rural life. And many of his followers appear distinguished for ignorance of the organic-biological bases of life, and also of the fact that the technical trend is exhaustive of both materials and men. The new Nazi dynamism has the same emphasis. Rauschning writes:

"It puts even the 'Blood and Soil' dogma out of date. That dogma, says Nickisch in his *Die Dritte Imperiale Figur,* published in 1935, is not a natural product 'but a romantic fancy. Where natural attachment to blood and soil has come to an end, it cannot be restored by a free decision.' The future of an 'uprooted nation,' and the German nation was one, like most of the nations of Europe for that matter, exists only in so far as it places 'its own versatility in its service' in penetrating the whole world. There is no way back to its roots. The desire to find a way back is almost evidence in itself of a feeling of being

[1] *Germany's Revolution of Destruction,* Wm. Heinemann, Ltd., London and Toronto.

too spent to be able to venture on the imperial flight into the wide world. This new versatility is dynamism.

"We are at the outset of a fresh world-start. This 'world technical trend,' says Nickisch, is inevitable. The capitalist world has worked its own ruin, it has delivered itself up to the process of self-destruction, in complete unconsciousness up to the moment of its fall, just like the *ancien regime* at the time of the French Revolution. But if the capitalist world is light-heartedly living for the profit of the moment, blind to the coming disaster as was the French feudal aristocracy, the 'technical ratio' is graver and more unemotional and more inexorable than any revolutionary tribunal. It establishes itself in indifference alike to opposition and to its own devoted advocates." [2]

If we take the foregoing as a true interpretation of the aims of tyrant states, we cannot fail to note a significant change in world-social theory. Industry is no longer to be the instrument of "lightheartedly living for the profit of the moment." Industry is to be the instrument of plain domination. Techno-tyranny is the latest named devil loose in the world.

It would be facile and superficial to blame the dictators for this. Had not the uprooting of populations, the drawing of people from land and property already taken place in the name of nineteenth-century progress? Nihilism (motion and excitement today and nothingness tomorrow) had already become the mark of the cities. Unemployment is one of the tidal products of nihilism. It was the uprooted populations, people re-

[2] *Op. cit.*, p. 73.

moved from property and self-employment, that made the world safe for dictatorships. Such people no longer know how to be free.

By our headlong urbanization we have been building the same nihilist structure in Canada and the United States. And if we escape the full blow of the hammer it is mainly because of our great riches and spaces. But we will be most blind and culpable if we do not hearken to the cackle of the geese.

Rauschning represents the Nazi as discarding the "Blood and Soil" idea for war and conquest, "imperial flight into the wide world." It may be said with truth that Hitler still talks of the sacredness of the peasantry. But that a land movement can no longer be stressed for Germany is clear. For urbanized populations dependent on war and war employment are precisely what is necessary to create the illusion that war must be waged. Neville Henderson, British Ambassador to Berlin, found that by 1938 sixty per cent or more of the sum of Germany's effort "in human beings, labor, and material was destined for war." [3] This kind of war-work, moreover, and the gearing of the whole economy to war is necessary to take up the slack in employment. War is part of such an economy. People are to be put to work to make instruments of destruction and to be destroyed. It is here that the nihilist character of the machine betrays itself.

The Soviets in their long campaign against war and fascism before 1939 had a lot to say about capitalism as a war-making system. This was the language of the

[3] *The Failure of a Mission*, Neville Henderson. G. P. Putnam's Sons, New York, 1940.

Communist for several years in his cells throughout the world. But the true character of industrialized Socialist Russia was not revealed. It took the opening of hostilities in Europe to do that, and Russia was seen to be as imperialistic a nation as any in history. Socialist Russia had become industrialized and urbanized. Although the anti-war note was strong in the doctrinaire part of Socialism, Russia could not deliver herself from the vices of capitalist societies. War seems to be an ultimate phase of the rhythm of centralized industrialism. Merely changing to Socialism only aggravates the tendency. The Socialist state—if it clings to centralism—is the nationalization of errors. And Communist criticism of war might become more valid if it recognized the organic as the roots of life and social policy.

Russian and German Socialism have produced examples of the centralized state. They have not shown the world anything that resembles the good society. The evils of techno-tyranny can be met in part by the awakening of an agrarian consciousness on a world scale. The harsher these evils become, the nobler and the more redemptive appears the example of the tiller on his yielding acres and the more urgent is the work of building the decentralist community. One feels that good men in all walks of life will see the mission, will defend the self-respect of rural living and promote rural institutions.

It is to be noted, according to this statement of Rauschning, that the Nazi looks upon the land movement as "romantic fancy." This is particularly to be marked; *it is exactly the attitude of the urbanized mind in all parts of the world.* It is not at all peculiar to Germany, or to any out-cropping of Socialist theory. It is precisely the attitude of most of our own educators and public men, even though they may occasionally drop a sentiment of regard for the "poor farmers." They do not follow the alternative through to its war-climax. It should indeed give pause to us, the people of the middle class, the way our shibboleths have of growing up suddenly into strange monsters! For "uprooted" peoples there is no way back to the roots. There is only war.

It cannot be overlooked that war's delirious enthusiasms and drastic processing of the human spirit help to make people vital again. Their willingness to suffer for their cause is not without its fruits. It may be that men who have learned to sleep on their haversacks, who have learned through war to be robust, will turn to land. The philosophers have sought for the moral equivalent of war. Materially speaking, it is hard to see how anything else than an agrarian restoration and the making of a rural culture can even partially fill the bill. And it is under somewhat epic dimensions that the new agrarianism would have the best chance to succeed.

The materialist mind sees in the land movement evidence of "being too spent" to venture into harsher conflicts. Only an "imperial flight into the wide world" can suffice. The whole thing is put into operation by a reversion to tribal collectivism under the leadership principle. Such is the drive in the machine that the future state of man is envisioned as one of permanent war. That this solution is sinister but appears more romantic than the land solution goes without saying.

What the Nazi mistakes for feebleness may be in

reality man's capacity to renounce impulsive action and give himself over to the maturities of meditation—to become mature in perception of values and freed from the frenzies of action without content. Dynamism can be a thing partly juvenile, partly diabolical.

Contrary to evidence of being too spent, the land movement represents vigor. It is, in fact, the moral cowardice in certain reform elements that shies away from land and localism, and misleads the masses into madcap and violent adventures. It takes more moral courage to clear one acre of land and shear your own sheep than it does to ride the bandwagon of the Party as an opinionless satrap of the Caesars. You have not only to plan, have faith and go at the work involved; you may also have to endure the disdain of an intelligentsia who have lost a true sense of the sacredness of common work.

It is true that there are sections of people too spent ever to matter in rural reconstruction. But the surrender to technical determinism implicit in the view that the technical "establishes itself in indifference alike to opposition and to its devoted advocates" is too much to swallow. In the Christian sense this burnt-out condition is no occasion for counsels of despair. Rather does it indicate the point of departure for a new start. A fresh world-start wholly under the banner of centralism would not be a fresh start, but an enlargement of what had already proved enfeebling, at least in the case of civilized societies.

Christianity has gone out to the barbarians in the past. It may be that Christianity will dig its trenches in the soil. The soil is where things grow. Or to state it

more correctly, the evils of techno-tyranny become so
evident that the Christian tradition will find an oppor-
tune time for the reassertion of its historical values
which had been ignored by liberalism and the rise of
capitalism. It seems to me that some of these are sum-
marized by Bernard Wall in the following words:

"It is impossible to love all mankind unless you
first love individual men, and unless your love goes
out in circles, always widening, from the family to
the locality, from the locality to the State, from the
State to the culture—in the sense that we all live in
our European culture—and then maybe to mankind
as a whole. The modern State has broken down local
culture, whether the French State of the Revolution
or the English commercial State; but this is an evil.
The left conception of humanity only accentuates the
evil to an immense degree, being born of the de-
racinateness of life—especially working and middle-
class life in the modern state. 'Universality is the
negation of cosmopolitanism,' wrote Miguel de Una-
muno, 'the more a man belongs to his own time and
country, the more will he belong to all times and all
countries.' " [4]

Commercialism broke down local culture. This re-
sulted in the breakdown of human initiatives locally
and dammed up the talents of people. This is one of the
great wastes attendant upon the so-called efficiency of
big industry. The most terrible wastes are those taking
down human values. The acceptance of war as a means

[4] From "Tradition and Social Justice," *The Dublin Review,* 1937.

to satisfy wants and fill the gap is a gesture that may bring glory to ambitious militarists and make temporary employment, but what does it mean to the great average of people whose aims are peace and security? The great rages of the Titans solve nothing. Society has to be repaired from the fringe—not in the dry-rotted centers. We fall or survive by what the common man does to reinstate himself in the conditions of liberty. When we get back to our roots, when we work for the revival of self-sufficiency at home—insofar as that is reasonable and scientific—we are taking the most effective action possible against the evils of statism. For in the same measure as you alleviate conditions in the local community, in an equal degree does the need of state-intervention decline.

Free America is the journal of the decentralist school of thought in the United States. This school of thought insists that decentralization is implicit in modern technology under free conditions. The trend, interrupted by war for the time being, is towards simplified machinery of a human and family scale. Mr. Ralph Borsodi, one of the editors, has done a great deal of practical research in the costs of things that can be produced in the rural home. He challenges centralism and furnishes documentation, which is supplied from experiments conducted under his supervision.

Borsodi has the honor of being one of the first economists seriously to challenge mass-production, so seriously that he lives in the country and has been seeking to establish experimentally ways to produce as much as possible in the farm home. He espouses part-time farming to produce for home use and is apparently bringing what to many had seemed an idle dream to proportions that draw the respect of even his enemies.

Small-scale production is cheaper, Borsodi claims, in all industries except those manufacturing automobiles, motors, electrical appliances, steel, wire, pipe, and similar goods. It was a mistake to shift production from the home to the factory. The savings through mass-production, except in the lines noted, are wiped out by the costs of distribution. These include: shipping (all the vast intricacies of transportation), warehousing, wholesaling, financing, selling (salesmen and retailers). An example: in 1929 the cost of factory-made flour was twice as high as that of custom-milled flour. The experiment appeals to people who have some income. A landward movement by even an intelligent minority would give an impetus to rural initiative and contentment.

Will overbuilt urban structures and mass-production centers be able to stand up to the eroding of low costs in the home and local-production sphere? It is worth noting that the greed that made centralism may yet take a hand in unmaking it—although this would be a doubtful ally to the true agrarians. Electricity will shortly be considered a necessity in rural communities. The making of small machines for household production, or for production of commodities by local co-operative groups, will be a field for the entrepreneur.

It is arguable that there is a connection between such use of machines and a revival of crafts and the artisan qualities in man. This is no doubt a debatable question. Grandfather lived on the farm in the age of crafts. In those days before the coming of any machine power, farm work included much drudgery. Today, heavy work can be done by machinery. The time thus saved should, in theory at least, give the man a chance to work at crafts in a much greater degree than was possible in the former days. And there are also crafts in connection with the use of machines. The trouble was that, with the coming of machinery, crafts were given up in favor of store-bought goods. The practice of craftsmanship lapsed. The machine to do slave work is here to stay. But craft work which involves creative satisfactions, self-development and self-provisioning in the absence of other gainful occupation should be here to stay also. It must be restored to its right, dignified place. For in some line and in some degree the artist is in every man. The freeing from slave work strengthens the possibility of crafts not only for use but also for beauty—for development of the individual's idea of beauty. This kind of thing taught and built up as a tradition in rural communities over a period of generations would be a main strand in the rural culture.

The war has changed some factors in social theory. Against totalitarian threats, all countries tend to become totalitarian. In darkness we change somewhat our democratic idea of the leadership principle. Force brings into being the principle of political authority that is above all economic and particular interests. States have need to become self-sufficient. This should help agriculture. The necessity of states having their people at work will in the future over-ride the dependence on imports in that degree known in the heyday of free trade. The tendency to national self-sufficiency may give impetus to self-sufficiency in the local community. What appear in war as substitutes often remain as standard products in peace.

The critics of decentralism will say that an industrially advanced and centralized nation can easily conquer an agricultural nation, can dominate it in the same way as the industrial North is alleged to have dominated the agrarian South in the United States. Whoever has the technical apparatus is easily master in war. But is there reason why an agricultural nation could not have as good a war machine as any? Given an equal armament, its strength of resistance would be in ratio to its decentralization of industry and population. The great centers of population make a nation weak and easily crippled. Under aerial attack the English said they were fifteen times safer in the country than they were in London. A decentralist nation would be, perhaps, fifteen times stronger than a centralized one. The greater the degree of economic sufficiency in the local community the greater the strength. Hence it is not far-fetched to say that building an indigenous rural economy and culture is, from the military standpoint, a step in the survival of free people.

In our opposition to totalitarianism we cannot overlook certain things. There are admissions we have to make. Societies which have withdrawn from local bodies the initiatives that are properly within the spheres of competence of local bodies are no longer democratic societies, no matter how zestfully they may cling to the franchise. In the economic sphere this withdrawal has taken place on a large scale. With the business of making things locally—that well could be made locally— went some of the substances of democracy. Unemployment is the proof and witness. The strong cherishing of the popular vote and the electing of representatives does not mean that all is well. A baby will cling even the more strongly to his bottle when the milk has disappeared from it.

Apart from the military field the front of a true social and economic order is in building the local community.

Through the many years of the expanding capitalist economy, labor unions defended the rights of man. Massed industry has now produced its ultimate in contradictions: technical plenty with an increase of poverty through unemployment. Mass unemployment is the reef upon which unionism is stranded. Fighting only for wages and tolerable conditions of work for a number of workers is a negative and rear-guard action. It is right in its scope, but it is negative because it is defending a diminishing rampart, for mass-production acts to displace further human work. The great labor unions are like hunters in a forest from which the quarry has flown. For a significant number of hopeful job-seekers the job is simply no longer there as it was in the period of the expanding industrial economy.

Labor needs to turn a corner and become positive again. It can become positive in its message by seeking to reconnect man with true productive property and with the conditions of personally responsible work wherein the faculties of the full human being are engaged. Only land is true property, being the vessel of the Life Force and under the law of increase when rightly used. All other forms of property are inferior to land, being under the law of depreciation. Labor action becomes positive also by having a spiritual content, by requiring of itself sacrifice for the re-establishment of the dignity of human work and by showing the road towards liberty—which to many of its followers can come only by decentralization.

Working-class leadership through unionism has tried to sell labor power; as an oversight it has neglected to husband the consumer power of its followers (in stores and credit unions and the establishments that come out of them) ; it has seemingly been ill-aware that the labor problem has its real roots in the non-use of land for family livelihood.

Working-class leaders have followed two types of action. One has had a fixation on the revolutionary mirage, or in its more moderate sector beat the tom-toms of political action—of political action *alone*. This could go only so far in a liberal democracy, for in the despiritualized state of modern society the economic power in the main determined the political power. Political action is one of the highways that lead to a better order. But is it the only one? Or is it the most important one? In that measure in which things are done by governments, in the exact same measure does the need of personal and co-operative initiative subside. We have to teach people to build the economic organizations that will save them. Their initiatives are primary. The more the secondary function is followed by governments the sounder is the social structure. But conditions have to be achieved and maintained which will permit personal and co-operative initiatives to be resultful so as to provide the good life. We have to seek an understanding of the complementary nature of government and of those organizations that are between it and the individual. This is the sphere of private associations. These are at their best when the sap of personal and free associative activity rises in them. These "move and live by the soul within them, and they may be killed by the grasp of a hand from without."

The second type of labor leadership had all its energies drawn into the struggle barely to hold the line in order to keep labor organization in existence at all. Labor leaders fought for better wages and better conditions of work. That they were unable to give the workers the vision and the organism of an evolutionary economic policy was certainly not their fault. They were subject to all the contagions of their environment. And both types of leader, even with all the petty racketeering and wild-eyed radicalism thrown in, do not escape their meed of honor. For in seeking to burst their own bondage they burst somewhat the bonds of others. Such men knew the haunting of insecurity and of thwarted imperatives within their hearts. If their motivations out-ran their knowledge others too were to blame for that.

This was labor in the era of individualism, the era in which education shied away from vital spots in human experience. The mind had retired from the hard job of devising forms which would enable the masses to acquire a partnership in the economic processes. Noble strides were made in almost every direction except that of devising forms which would implement justice as between man and man. But was it an inertia of the mind alone? Was it not also a stay of the spirit fearful that even if the forms were devised men would not have the vision and the zeal to put them into action?

In some countries labor has become merely a department in the totalitarian set-up. On this side of the water,
if labor clings to negative policies it may meet the same
fate. But if it should become positive and come alive
with a full-bodied philosophy of work and be a maker
of rural and decentralizing institutions it would mitigate
the rigors of the impending encroachments of the state
upon individual liberties.

In the absence of effective reforms set in motion by
working-class leaders, the reforms come at last from
some other source. Perhaps no longer can it be honestly
said that it is a race between the moralist and the man
who is given charge. More people than ever will ap-
prove today these words of Salazar:

> "The state must be strong, but it must be limited
> by the demands of morality, by the principles of
> men's rights, by individual guarantees and liberties,
> which are the first and foremost condition of social
> solidarity. The state must be a man of honor."

PART 2

The Co-operative Estates of the Future
as an Instrument
of a Decentralist and Human Order

CHAPTER VI

Co-operatives and Credit Unions

THE ideas touched in the foregoing pages may be said to have to do with the soul of rural life. They suggest, roughly and incompletely, a background of thought and feeling about the rural environment. They suggest ideas vital and necessary to set the heart true, but they have not much gruel in them: they have not enough forceful material substance to set in motion landward progress on a scale to meet the demands.

The history of land-settlement efforts up to now rather go to prove this. The philosophical background is important. There are also a vast set of religious motivations that enter into the equation in view of the fact that the crisis in society is a moral crisis. The Christian dynamic of the "little way" is a secret weapon not matched in the armory of the proud masters of the world, nor apt to thrive best in the pride of the cities.

Socially conceived, the little way is the village way of life. It is a way that has deeply rich and subtle values. Christ was a man of the villages. Tolstoy struck his great chords in his love for the littleness of the peasant. When he had illiterate folk gathered in his house people thought that he was teaching them something. Tolstoy replied that he was not teaching them anything. He was trying to learn from them. From the case history of the common man we learn what is wrong —or what is right—with the world.

Interest in human beings is one of the strengths of

the village. And it is only upon a kindly and constructive interest in human beings that a truly human culture can be built. The dispersed attention and the impersonalism of our urban and mechanized lives are rapidly turning us into warrens of barren fools. We are so taken with motion that we pass up man. "The ill from which we are suffering," said Eric Gill, "is the decay of personality. The remedy is the revival of personal property."

The village of the future should be a human-scale community. One of the principal aims should be to deliver people from being crushed by the tyranny of the stimuli about them. We do not have to look far back to see such an order in existence. Less than sixty years ago there was in most parts of the United States and Canada a thriving local life, made up of activities that can only roughly be compounded in the meaning of the word *localism*. Motors, industrialization, the view that progress meant getting away from the land, the lack of an agrarian economy and culture affirmed by our educators and implemented by our governments— all this did for us what the enclosures plus industrialism did for England. In North America people have been leaving the rural villages before any enclosure system even threatened; but it is coming fast now in the form of industrial farming.

It was in England that the village, nurtured through centuries, came to that richness in human values which Goldsmith knew and which accounted for his intense feeling. "The sad historian of the pensive plain," he himself recorded the outraged sense of English common men as the Industrial Revolution completed what the

Enclosure Acts had begun. A long, hard, losing battle had been fought before Goldsmith gave tongue to the folk-soul of England.

Villagers before the fourteenth century had had a form of democracy, based on common land, which puts to shame the shibboleths and hypocrisy of our day. The economy was a combination of agriculture and crafts. The open-field system and communal land for grazing kept the avaricious from getting rich and provided easy access for the young to a livelihood according to the standards of the time. As the landlords came to power, their will became more overbearing. In 1381 the cry of the villagers was: "We are men formed in Christ's likeness and we are kept like beasts." [1] That was the voice of Christianity defying the lords. Christians, themselves, in such a locale were not entombed in property. In the sixteenth century, says Massingham, the village was insurgent. "In the nineteenth, it feebly twisted in its winding sheet."

The several stages of enclosure had made a trade empire and ruined the core of the English nation.

And what type of man, you will ask—and here is the real test—was produced by that co-operative village culture of Old England? He was not the broken relic of a culture that we see too often today: the being from whom crafts have been removed, pride of place destroyed, use of local materials seized, zest and vital spirit departed. No. He was man audaciously alive in the skills and disciplines of his independence. It was in the generations of villagers that was incubated the

[1] H. J. Massingham, "Our Inheritance from the Past," an article in the book, *Britain and the Beast,* London, 1938, J. M. Dent & Sons.

iron that is in the English character today. Massingham describes the men of the villages:

"The men who knew thirteen hundred ways of telling you you were a fool, and from whom Shakespeare quarried a thousand nuggets of speech; the men whose seasonal rituals and junketings, whose feasts and fairs and folk-lore echo to this day in the nursery; the men who tanned their own leather, built their own ploughs and wagons, wove their own clothing from flax and fleece, brewed their own beer, baked their own bread, cured their own bacon, built and thatched and decorated their own homesteads with the art the moderns try to preserve in the old villages; practised the time-honoured crafts in their own parish; conducted their own government and made the very spoons and mugs from which they ate and drank so heartily—were these the ancestral stock of the slouching, Victorian nondescript who pulled his cap as Lady Bountiful rode by in her brougham? Why was Weyhill celebrated for its cheeses? Why were the villages at the knees and under the arm-pits of the downs built of chalk, flint, and 'clunch,' and those of the Cotswolds and Northamptonshire of that limestone that takes the winds and suns and frosts with beauty? Why do the architectural styles of our ancient villages vary according to their regional grouping, and how comes it that each one of them reflects the geological formation, the natural configuration, and even the vegetation of its particular locality? Why, in other words, are they inevitably beautiful by the only aesthetic law that matters, the law of fitness to environment? It is hard for us to understand these things who are so well equipped by mass-production that our red-brick villas equally scale the Pennines as edge the Saxon shore. It is hard for us who are governed by the lowest common multiple of uniformity in speech, in clothes, in food, in all things, to envisage the spirit of local particularity. But the answer to all these and similar questions is the village community which was murdered by the grandfather of our own Machine Age—the enclosures."

The villages were small. Everybody knew everybody else. Everybody was close to the soil as a base of subsistence and was, therefore, in possession of a substantial degree of independence. Bureaucracy could be kept to a minimum. It is only in such a human-scale community that a social ideal is workable. Massingham says of the economic life of the village:

"The constitution of the village community effected an extraordinarily stable balance between socialism and ownership. Its governing body was the open-air assembly, meeting at a place sanctified by tradition and electing its own annual officers by popular and unanimous vote—the viewers, the common shepherd and herdsman, the pinder for straying cattle, the hayward, the chimney-sweeper, the reeve, the provost, and others. Even those natives more specialized and less intimate with the seasonal routine of agriculture—the smiths, the millers, the bee-keepers, the carpenters, bricklayers, masons, bakers, and fishermen—were, as members of a self-acting, self-sufficing, and self-governing local organism, granted holdings in the village fields in return for their services to the community. Graft, intrigue, bureaucracy, over-specialization, and other familiar evils that accompany national or imperial administration in the modern sense must surely have been kept in check by the free human contacts between man and man, the lack of financial incentive in the daily round, the bonds of traditional observance, the absence of social division and enmity, and the deep attachment of one and all to the land of their birth, their work and their village. Freeholders and customary tenants, all were children of the genius of place. Modern socialism, being a machine similar in structure if differing in policy and principle from the existing machine of national government, cannot even conceive the nature of a society repeated, with a wide range of variations in detail, thousands of times over. In them, diversity of employment among all took the place of standardization; custom and common agreement of authority and law, and individual though not private ownership of the land, existed within the framework of a co-operative system. With farm servants and day labourers, but no landless proletarian class, the village community did accomplish the to us incredible feat of reconciling independence with interdependence, and tradition with the free play of the individual within the body of the village. Those limits could hardly have been very exacting when much of the art, most of the architecture, and all of the craftsmanship of the Middle Ages rose out of the free township and the 'manorial' village. Its great disadvantages were

the occurrences of famine owing to natural dispensa-
tions and the lack of open communications more
onerous in medieval than, curiously enough, in pre-
historic times."

In the co-operative village of Tompkinsville in Cape
Breton, Nova Scotia, miners are using land both as
individuals and as a group. They have similar plans for
the development of crafts. Villa Nova, another recently
established co-operative village of miners, is studying
the community milling of flour, and the men are looking forward to the use of the land. Co-operative work
in the village gives outlet to creative energies and
brings an added interest to local living.

Recently, the Rev. Huber Duren of Westphalia, Iowa,
told a rural-life meeting at St. Cloud, Minnesota, what
co-operatives were doing among his parishioners. Five
musical organizations had been formed and co-operative
athletic teams had been champs. "There are 40,000
communities in this country like Westphalia," he said.
"They can do what we have done in Westphalia, and
if they would get busy and do it, we would quickly
solve our problems. We estimate and we can prove that
at least $15,000 is now being saved and kept in West-
phalia through our co-operatives and that money was
being sucked away and into New York and Chicago.
It was the life blood of our people. Had it continued,
we would have died."

It is only a little over a century since England's rich
village life was swept away. Village living still exists, of
course, in all countries. But in North America it has
lacked sufficiently strong champions in our literary,

educational and political circles. Perhaps the form can be brought back to life. Its most devouring enemy has been in the economic realm. It is above all necessary to throw up great economic institutions that will act for this rural village economy and culture.

For a rural culture there are many beliefs and attitudes that must be given to the individual. There are many forms of local production that can be re-established. There is the personal integrity that goes with the spirit of work, the solvency and skills that go with home-use production. All these must be retained. But can the agrarian community cut itself off from the heritage of the great, wide world? If it did, could it expect to hold its youth? In preserving the specific character of local things that are good few will advocate isolation. Space is conquered; the world today is a small one. Contact with the outside world is a necessity. In certain lines mass-production cannot be challenged. The most avowed agrarian goes beyond his community for many things.

In the business life there are many contacts with the outside, but very frequently in a way that is inimical to rural morale. One type of business offers hope: the co-operative. The co-operatives have a social outlook and in many cases are aware of the problems of our day. They are in the hands of the people. Taken all together they can be seen as a great estate of the rank and file. It may be that the co-operative estates are destined to become the physical body, to give solidarity and economic fecundity to the whole ruralizing process.

We may glean something of the far reflexes of Co-operation from these words of Dr. Coady:

"Co-operation will give the people a measure of economic independence but it will do something infinitely greater than this. It will condition them to the point where they are able to manipulate effectively the other forces that should operate in a democratic society. The process by which they achieve this will toughen their sinews and make them worthy of the good society when it does emerge. It will do so by stimulating the intellectual activity of the people and giving them a new interest in civic affairs.[2]

Dr. Coady has always held up the moral function of co-operatives as a force quite apart and above the immediate material gain they may effect in any community. There is the big picture that previsions co-operative institutions as foci of true social outlook, the viewpoint that holds the good of the community before the right to riches of the fortunate individual. By means of co-operatives, he has always held, the common people can achieve economic influence, and can be conditioned to the point from which they can the more easily meet whatever other problems are pressing on them. Since the breakdown of solidarity and the rise of individualism the people have not been able to realize their power.

This breakdown took place through the period of the Industrial Revolution. Anyone who doubts this should make a study of the inflections of capitalism that have crept, imperceptibly perhaps, into education, literature, political thought, and most flagrantly into radio and journalism. Modern journalism is a very

[2] *Masters of Their Own Destiny*, Harpers, New York, 1939, p. 125.

costly business and can be carried on only by tapping moneyed sources. Even the manifest honesty of most editors is not capable of breaking out of the strait-jacket and formulating policies that could cope with the decay, the weakness, and the stupidities of the age.

Apparently the same thing applies to radio. With land-use and home-use production so obviously a wholesome way out for many stranded and jobless people, radio is mostly given over to programs which, in effect, persuade the people to do none of these things, but on the contrary persuade them that they must buy lotions to keep their palms soft, they must buy pink pills to keep their digestive juices active, they must buy rub-on and buy rub-off, and they must generally keep chasing their tails in order that all kinds of goods may be sold to them. That all this adds up to an anti-social program and to consequent decadence never seems to have occurred to anyone. The commercialist mind lags twenty years behind social realities. To admit its weakness is bad for its business.

Co-operatives can muster the economic means to start the propagation of a true popular economy and culture by means of education, literature, radio and journal-ism. That is their tremendous far-reaching significance at this time. Thus the co-operatives, if infused with the true agrarian outlook and purpose, can be a very powerful sponsor of the reunion of man and land, of the recognition, on the part of all, of the nihilism that attaches to endless technicalization, and of the realization of the truth that the reservoirs of life are in the biological and organic forces.

It is true that co-operatives in all countries have not

done this and met their challenge. In England two great consumer societies and their branches alone do an annual business of about twenty-six million pounds. Their consumer-owned activities include many departments of modern merchandising. The Co-operative Wholesale Society is one of the greatest businesses in the country. Several journals are dedicated to the service of the movement. Much literature and educational and even political effort is carried on. Yet it is not evident that the English movement has put in motion an effective agrarian program; it has done noble work, but it is not clear that it had the purpose of delivering Englishmen from proletarian decline.

In the Scandinavian countries, on the contrary, co-operatives had become the strong arm of rurality. In Finland tenantry had been reduced from sixty per cent to nine per cent in twenty years. Likewise in Denmark, Sweden, and Norway, the co-operatives became one of the means of reconnecting man with property, with self-employment and personally responsible and creative work. But the societies were flanked by an effort at making a consciously rural culture. The economic co-operatives can become the arm of truth and give substance to social ideals.

I do not believe that a consumers' establishment which becomes merely another prop of already over-centralized and over-built urban structures will serve fully the quest for the true human order. That it can do a great deal of good is obvious. But in North America the co-operative estates if they are to be the spearhead of a really great folk-movement should steer agrarian. This, of course, is easier said than done; our most socially-minded people are of the industrial wage-class, most of the money is in the towns and cities, and co-operative stores and credit unions soon build good commercial structures in this environment. But how they can become anything much more than commercial structures is not clear. True co-operatives depend upon community spirit, upon building that sense of the community—a procedure on which George Russell, the Irish seer of rural Co-operation, placed such stress. This sense of the community is hardly possible under the conditions of modern urbanism. A community is much more than merely the physical juxtaposition of persons.

But urban co-operatives can serve a tremendous function when they become centers of an agrarian and decentralist outlook—as distinct from the centralist and collectivist outlook—and when they foster institutions to that end. In Maritime Canada, credit and consumer societies grow fastest in towns and cities where there is a large wage income. It is from such a growth among those who have that the movement gets strong in business contacts and agencies of education to fight the battles of those who have not in the sparsely populated regions. This is not only sensible business, it is also of the nature of Charity; it is germane to the co-operative set-up. Those who would isolate the movement in rundown areas can hardly expect to build a great movement.

There is, however, the difficulty to be faced of giving urban societies this decentralist outlook. If they do not move in this direction they move in the opposite, for the politics of over-centralized populations is trending to statism. Murray Lincoln has outlined the difference between American Co-operation and Socialism. He writes:

"People can fashion any kind of economic system they want. We must remodel the economic system as we know it. But we can still have private ownership, private enterprise, and civil liberties, and this does not mean socialism. Cooperation is the very antithesis of socialism. In socialism, all economic activities are carried on by the government bureaus. In cooperation, they are carried out voluntarily by the people themselves. And this is most important for cooperators to appreciate and understand—for the major political trend in the world is towards socialism, including the good old U. S. A." [3]

Adult education in Maritime Canada has shown that a strong financial estate of the people can be built through credit unions, provided there is some regional educational institution willing to do the job. Since 1933, three hundred and sixty-six credit unions have been started. It is the mobilization of thrift. It is an enlivening experience to find that, by gathering up the crumbs, by putting aside the nickels and dimes that would otherwise be frittered away, a people's estate can be built up with good effects upon character and morale. The founders of this credit union network now look forward to the formation of a long-term credit institu-

[3] *The Producer, Political and Purchasing Approach to Economic Problems,* an address delivered by Murray D. Lincoln, secretary, Ohio Farm Bureau Cooperative Association, at the Twelfth Biennial Congress and Silver Anniversary Celebration of The Cooperative League of the U. S. A., Hotel Morrison, Chicago, October 16-18, 1940.

tion which will be able, free of government aid, to finance land settlement, rural and urban housing. This is one of the prospects of the future. The few dollars that are being put aside month by month will make up the reserve by which sons and younger brothers will, in years to come, be enabled to buy land or build a house. How often has the cry—"If I had the capital"— been like a prayer and a sigh on the lips of farmless farmers, of homeless and defeated men! A credit institution that will answer this prayer of the people for land and home can be built through credit unions. In this region alone there are now fifty thousand members, most of whom are putting aside their bit in the credit union estate.

Habits of thrift, knowledge of group techniques, community spirit, educative contacts, responsibilities and practical gains—these are immediate advantages of the credit union. The practical gains by having a ready source of short-term credit in the neighborhood are manifold. Especially is this true of the rural sections. Credit unions promote planning. Their rules are that loans should be made for provident and productive purposes. This fits excellently into rural possibilities. The credit union should be marked as the financial instrument of a *provident* culture. This again shows their close natural hook-up with a rural philosophy. The rural terrain is the provident terrain; and the slow sound growth of credit and, in fact, of all co-operative societies is in keeping with an organic tempo.

Land use in most areas makes possible a great diversity of enterprise. For the average farmer it is small enterprise. A workable but safe system of credit is required. The credit union is most admirably fitted to the needs of the small producer. In its practical working-out many examples could be cited. One that comes to mind is that of a farm family in one of the eastern counties of Nova Scotia. The man was in ill-health and the wife was hard pushed to support the family. At one time in 1937 the family came down to their last dollar. A credit union had recently been set up in the community. The woman actually took their last dollar and joined. She at once borrowed and bought turkey poults and what feed was needed to carry them up to the time of marketing. That fall their turkeys were top grade and the family netted six hundred dollars cash. In such cases the credit union implements unused and creative forces in both land and human character. One gets a glimpse of potentially great and diverse forces that slumber in this sound but ready harnessing of credit and land. This harnessing of group-solidarity in a concrete way is helpful in bringing out the productive properties of land.

What applies to tillers holds also for fishermen. In L'Ardoise on the Cape Breton shore, mackerel fishing is a leading occupation. A young man who came from Halifax had married a girl in this village. He joined the fishermen's society and started to fish mackerel. The young couple wanted living quarters, and occupation of a house and property could be secured for the down payment of fifty dollars—which the man did not have. He, therefore, asked the manager of the Fishermen's organization to advance the amount.

"There are two hundred men in this Co-op," the manager said. "If we should advance fifty dollars to each, what would become of our operating capital! But I think the credit union should fix you up."

Together they went to the credit union and the loan was secured. The man's unsold fish was security. The young couple moved into their new home. They think co-operation is a very good thing.

A member of the New Waterford Credit Union wanted to buy a stove, price $120. He had $70.00 in the Credit Union. He could offer the merchant the $70.00 cash with the promise to pay $2.00 weekly until the stove was his. The retailer could not lower the price any on this instalment basis. But the prospective customer found out that the cash price was 20 per cent less. So he borrowed $100 from the Credit Union, paid it back at the rate of $2.00 weekly and added 25 cents each week to his shares.

When the loan was gradually repaid, the credit union member had not only the stove but $84.75 to his credit.

Instances like these show the societies at work in the interests of little folk. One wonders, if credit unions had been here from the start—from the first settlers— would the exodus from the land have been so marked in later times? Not having an obvious source of credit, the tiller acquired too easily the habit of going in debt to the merchants. The farmstead soon began to go down. I can remember it was always this same story which the wise old men were giving as the cause of the breakdown of rural livelihood twenty-five years ago. This "getting in debt" on the farm was what prepared the way for the move to town to seek a wage-job.

Merchants themselves in some cases realize this. In Nova Scotia the co-operative stores are trying to get the people away from store credit. Last fall a private store-owner commented to this writer on the point:

"There is one thing I like about the co-operative movement," he said; "that is their stand against credit. I have observed for some years the evils that credit brings to certain types of people. If they can get groceries on credit they will do so and bank on something turning up in three or six months' time which will give them the chance to earn the money to pay for the groceries. As a result of being able to buy on credit they have not planned ahead. They put off bestirring themselves to meet the bill until in time they get in too deep. In rural people with the means of producing many of the things they buy, or if not that of producing something of value with which to meet their necessary expenses, this attitude is hard to excuse. But the system of giving credit has got them into it. I see now that it is a far better thing to go out and try to teach such people how to get along without getting in debt, to show them how buying on credit is their loss and everyone's loss in the end. Buying on credit accounts for many an abandoned farm. It cripples and puts to sleep something in a man. A change is overdue."

The credit union can play a great role in rural revival. Out in Africa the Rev. Bernard Huss championed the cause of these societies for the natives. The white man's individualism had begun to affect them. Friends of the Negro saw it wise to retain that sense of community which had been strong in the tribes. The native tradition was that only such wealth would be permitted as did not jeopardize the good of the tribe. This tradition had behind it a record of drastic enforcements. If a member of the tribe grew too rich and neglected his responsibilities to others, he could be accused of amassing wealth by witchcraft. He could be eaten by the chief of the tribe. "This," Father Huss wrote, "was a very crude but effective method of preserving social equality. No one could get rich at the expense of others, there was no possibility of 'get down that I may get up.' "

Father Huss wrote a book [4] in which he sought to tie up this old native community-sense with credit unions. He embodied in his book the experience and principles of Raiffeisen, the founder of co-operative credit. Raiffeisen had insight into human character. He knew how circumstance could warp and twist the man. He refuted the impression still often heard—that the poor and ignorant are a hopeless lot and nothing can be done with them. "We often hear the words," he wrote, "that there is absolutely nothing to be done with this pack. It is too lazy, too stupid, too suspicious. Such statements are to be condemned. We can do something with any man if we treat him in the right way and have the necessary patience." His first care was to train persons to be co-operators. The all-important thing was the right spirit. This he found in the words of Christ: "Amen, I say to you, as long as you did it to one of my least brethren you did it to Me." There was none of the brackish water of atheistic humanitarianism in this father of the credit union—which in less than one

[4] *People's Banks,* Rev. Bernard Huss, Mariannhill, Natal, Africa.

hundred years has pushed into all the frontiers of the world. He knew the true source of the lesser loves; his humanism was centered in the all-High, and it came all the deeper down, and with ease, into the tortuous human depths.

Have the necessary patience. That, in the view of this present writer, is one of the chief keys to success in building credit unions or any other kind of co-operatives. The persons in charge of the practical organizing work for a given region must be possessed of exceptional patience. Endless repetition, endless committee work, endless entanglements with unpredictable elements in human character—all these come upon the man in charge. He must teach the societies how to operate as successful business units. Yet he must not show the slightest cynicism. Nothing is more fatal to the co-operative spirit, for it is on a certain cynicism that individualist business is built. And it is upon cynicism, full-grown, that tyrants build their empires. Co-operation, if it is to matter greatly, will seek to enrich people by drawing out the hidden better self. This is delicate piloting. Here angels fear to tread. Here only the inward stuff of Christianity can cope with what comes up. Some years ago I remember reading that a certain economic reform effort in England failed; the reason given was that the endless committee work proved too monotonous to the instigators. I think many earnest people are suspicious of Co-operation for this same reason.

In Nova Scotia credit union growth has been fast. It was only in December 1933, that the first ones were set up as a result of the efforts of Dr. M. M. Coady and

A. B. MacDonald. The author is not here essaying to give the full history of credit union origins in the Province.[5] At present there are 196 credit unions in Nova Scotia with assets of $887,635. The organizing of this seven-year-old brood has been one of the activities of A. B. MacDonald, Associate Director of the University of St. Francis Xavier Extension Department, who is Managing Director of the League, and whose judicious mind and creative patience have carried such benefits all through the Maritime Movement.

Many people in local communities take part in starting and guiding these societies. Too much praise cannot be given to those shapers of new instruments of welfare who see the vision and are seized with the desire to "clean up their corner of creation." It must be that some inner voice informs them of the value of their work. The experience they obtain is, of course, educational. The people's economic societies are excellent schools of citizenship.

The rank and file have suffered a great deal through lack of a group-discussion technique. So solid is the selfishness of human nature that the sufferings of those who remain silent will go unseen and will run to intolerable lengths. Brother Francis of Assisi, the famed friend of the poor, thought that the poor had the duty to make known their plight. Unfortunately in our day the custom is that the poor remain silent until they become incensed; then their representations seem to savor of revolution or are usable by fomenters of revo-

[5] Dr. J. J. Tompkins had in 1924 corresponded with the Carnegie Corporation, Roy Bergengren and others about Credit Unions. Rev. R. L. MacDonald as President of the Nova Scotia Farmers' Ass'n brought the idea before that body in 1925.

lution. Thus a great many people who are only poor and inexpert at expressing their rights are maneuvered into the position where they look like Bolsheviks. Good group-discussion methods enable people to meet, to thresh out their grievances, to study their economic needs, and to formulate plans to overcome their difficulties and present them in an orderly way to the powers that be. Such group-discussion is an integral part of credit-union education. It should also greatly help working-class people to defend their meetings from the railroading proclivities of those who would slant opinion towards subversive ends.

Credit unions can be of special value to rural life. Where farmers are close together a sense of community comes easily. In the towns, conditions make people more competitive. Where the farmers have not built and learned how to use credit unions they have frequently to buy their groceries from the merchant on credit and are thus committed to sell their produce to him. The amount of bargaining power they have is nil, and if it is figured out it becomes clear why people who have to do this stay very poor always. Credit to the well-to-do is one thing, but credit of this kind moves towards slavery.

"It sounds like a paradox but it is nevertheless true that some people suffer harm because they do borrow money, while others suffer harm because they do not borrow money. Here is the explanation of this seemingly queer statement. Ignorant, foolish and lazy people suffer harm because they borrow money improvidently, extravagantly and unproductively. They do not know better, and as long as they have property to lose, money-lenders are willing to lend them money without inquiring into the purpose of the loan; they are in fact delighted to see the debt mount up and often they do not even desire the repayment of the principal, they are just content to live on the interest while keeping the debtor just alive and in despair. In this depressed condition the poor and uneducated man, quite ignorant of the cause of his trouble and hopeless of escape, becomes dishonest and demoralized. The small farmer in particular is exposed to these perils of credit: his labor gives him a return not weekly or monthly, but often only after six months, and in the event of bad harvests, after a year or more. He hardly keeps accounts and is slow to adopt new methods or act on skilled advice. On the other hand there are many poor simple people who suffer loss because they are afraid to borrow money or are unable to borrow any money or to borrow it on reasonable terms, or do not borrow enough money for productive work." [6]

Credit unions are spreading throughout Canada. Quebec has an established movement started by Desjardins, and seems to have offset effectively the idea that poor parishes cannot raise considerable sums over a good period of time. The short-sighted critic will say with an air of finality: "How can the people save in this poor village? They have no money." At first blush it looks strange. But if you figured out what these people had paid in interest on loans for ten or fifteen

6 *Op. cit.*, p. 5.

years, you would find that they were supporting a credit structure but not owning it. And in not owning it they had passed up an instrument of influence and defense in the realm of opinion and ideas.

It was at Levis, Quebec, on December 8, 1900, that the first "caisse populaire" was formed by Desjardins, who was also the original founder of the credit unions now operating in the United States. By 1938 there were 393 societies operating in the Province. In thirty-five years their loans had amounted to $200,000,000. Their losses during the period were only one-twentieth of one per cent. If the interest which these people of humble means paid back to themselves on this $200,-000,000 were figured, and if there were added to that the additional interest they would have had to pay if the loans were procured from loan-sharks, the enormous significance of this good community-housekeeping will be seen.

The provinces of Ontario, Saskatchewan, British Columbia and Manitoba, and the Island of Newfoundland are all now bringing up a thrifty young flock of credit unions. Little Prince Edward Island has 46 unions with almost complete coverage of her area. New Brunswick has 124 with 17,000 members. If the Canadian movement keeps on growing under wise guidance it will soon add up to a worthwhile estate. It is at least one phase of education for common men and women to learn how to handle their own financial affairs and keep control of what they earn and save.

Credit unions in the United States have reached formidable size. At the eleventh annual meeting of the Iowa Credit Union League Mr. Thomas Doig, Assistant

Managing Director of the Credit Union National Association, reviewed the movement. There were, he said, 8,400 credit unions in the country, serving 2,000,000 persons, and having assets of over 220 million dollars. The Nova Scotia Credit Union League in the 1940 annual meeting voted to affiliate with CUNA which is now an international organization.

It is true that credit unions grow fastest in industrial centers. But it is clear that the rural flank of the development, with its numbers and the variety of its uses, offers great promise. It is one of the main arteries in the future agrarian body. Through its stream can be carried vital concepts of land, work and culture.

CHAPTER VII

The Consumer Establishment

FOR poor people one of the easiest routes to share-partnership in the economic processes is through the co-operative store. Local people in the neighborhood, by pooling their spending power, build a business for themselves. This business, the co-operative store, joins with others of its kind and they form a wholesale organization. The wholesale in time, when its volume is built up, can enter the production field in certain lines. If the stores are largely rural ones the wholesale may already have introduced marketing systems for the small primary producers—as is the case of Maritime Co-operative Services at Moncton and Sydney. Or in any case, as the purchasing power of the wholesale becomes large it can stand for a just price for farm produce. This is a function of tremendous significance.

The very great place of the co-operative store in the rural program cannot be overlooked. A good many rural advocates put all their eggs in one basket and espouse producer co-operatives alone. This seems to be the first stage of becoming experienced in rural economics. But men who have spent many years in the movement are more and more emphasizing the consumer approach. It is true that tillers have to produce before they can get money to buy things. And where cash incomes are very low it is natural and right to start producer societies. But to produce profitably it is necessary to buy certain things economically; that means consumer business, for although the consumer society will trade at market prices the wide effect on the price structure is by no means negligible, as countless examples show. As the consumer societies become strong they may set prices that are just for all parties.

The co-operative stores, too, can provide the business contacts, the wholesaling facilities, the trained businessmen who know both ends of the game. Most important of all they are able, through their provision for education, to build up a school of thought that can bring into being a full-bodied program of Co-operation. The producer co-operative has a limited appeal, usually specializing in some one product, and not taking in all the people. Often, too, the product is a seasonal one. The members want to get all they can for what they sell. All in all, the conditions for building a community spirit are not at their best and most constant in the producer co-operative.

This is not in any sense to minimize the importance of the producer and marketing organizations. It is merely to reassert that the sure and good way to build them is in collaboration with an evolving consumer establishment—provided that the latter has a genuine agrarian slant. That is most important. In the Maritimes we do not believe that the people who are trying to revive widespread rural ownership and land-use will get very far without building co-operative stores and wholesales. The consumer units have fecundity, their power of growth is well proven. They should be able, in the course of time, to build a business framework and to create a body of opinion that will support small ownership and rural causes all along the line.

If agrarians ignore this they will leave their other efforts exposed to the same forces that got us in the ditch that we are in. Was it not, in large part, the forces of capitalist commercialism that set up the attitudes and the sense of values that sent so many people away from the land? It is not merely a matter of how much the people may be out of pocket in their business deals; it is what leverage does the ownership of businesses give for the propagation of the socially right attitudes and values. Therein lies one of the great promising features of consumer enterprises.

Small rural producers have been more or less oblivious of the fact that they were paying tribute to big companies that sold them machinery, feed, clothing, furniture and a dozen other things. They have been slow to realize that they made these big companies what they are. Through their stores they could use their money to build their own estate. Provided there is guidance and study-club work it can be done. To say that they are not capable of doing this can no longer be credited. They can hire good talent for much less than what it now costs them. They could hire some of the same types of men who, in the absence of Co-operation, go into private business, and these latter would like it for they would have a chance to make a fair living according to their talents and at the same time help to build business estates of the people with a social conscience.

"Factories are free." This actually comes true when consumers run stores. The people in some places through their wholesales now jointly own factories.

This ownership has cost them nothing, except faith, study, and a sense of brotherhood.

Murray D. Lincoln, of the Ohio Farm Bureau, has been for many years a student of rural economic problems. Recently he wrote:

"Since producer organization has no control over the consumer market, it is obviously ineffectual. It may possibly eliminate one set of profit-takers, but still leaves the producer helpless against others. The failure of the poultry and egg program to solve the producers' difficulties in our state is a good example of this. In Ohio the egg marketing program has lost money simply because of its lack of control of the ultimate market for its products. All it has been able to do is eliminate some of the speculators' profits, make improvements in quality and full measure. I believe in producer action, but without market control it is futile.

". . . Consumer action, by organizing the market first, starts at the place that will ultimately solve our marketing problems.

". . . You and I exercise absolute control over where we buy a suit of clothes, a basket of groceries, or a tractor, plow, feed, seed or fertilizer. Thus, a few people banding together can operate a buying cooperative, because they dictate the channels through which their buying power becomes effective.

". . . Have you ever stopped to realize that it is your seemingly insignificant daily purchase of groceries, clothes, fuel, your payment of insurance premiums and bank deposits, that support the vested commercial and financial institutions of our country? The only way to reform our economic system is to mobilize our buying power through co-operative channels and thus remove this tribute and support from those who exploit us with our own money." [1]

Mr. Lincoln referred to an article on *Farm Income* in the October 1937 issue of *Fortune* in which it is shown that the farmer in the United States spends twenty-six per cent more for the consumer needs of the family than he spends for the farm. This suggests that rural people should not only buy co-operatively things like feed and fertilizers that have to do with the farm, but should also enter the larger field of household and family requirements. On the basis of $10,000,000,000, *Fortune* estimated 1937 expenses as follows:

For the Farm

Taxes, interest, repayment of loans	$ 1,000,000,000
Feed, seed, fertilizer	750,000,000
Insecticides, containers, twine	120,000,000
Farm machinery and repairs	550,000,000
Automobiles and trucks	350,000,000
Farm Buildings and repairs	280,000,000
Cash wages for hired labor	600,000,000
Cost of operating autos, tractors, and trucks	470,000,000
Miscellaneous	130,000,000
	$ 4,250,000,000

For the Farmer

Store-bought food	$ 1,610,000,000
Clothing	1,150,000,000
House furnishings	860,000,000

[1] "A Study of the Producer-Consumer Relations," *Rural America*, April, 1939.

Recreation, charity, gifts, etc. ....$ 1,040,000,000
Medical and dental   400,000,000
General household operation (fuel, light,
  telephone, ice, repairs and improvements
  to house and grounds, etc.)   570,000,000
Savings (insurance, etc.)   120,000,000
                                        ─────────────
                                        $ 5,750,000,000

Total $10,000,000,000

If rural people bought their household goods alone [2] through their own co-operative stores they could save $74,100,000 yearly, Mr. Lincoln estimated. The figures in the above tables are rather staggering. Some of the items, like wages for hired labor and medical care, can be left out; a further substantial discount could be made for home-use production. Enough remains to indicate that if even a considerable part of this business were carried on through rural-consumer channels a strong decentralizing force could be brought into play, provided the leaders recognized the need, at this time, of a positive agrarianism.

Fathers Rawe and Ligutti have called attention to certain figures given by Paul W. Stewart and J. Frederic Dewhurst in the book by the two latter men, *Does Distribution Cost Too Much?*:

"In their studies of distribution, Stewart and Dewhurst found that the multiple processing and transportation throughout the economic system results in a tremendous turnover of the same goods. For example, in the year 1929, $12,400,000,000 of agricultural products, $4,900,000,000 of mineral products, and $4,400,000,000 of general imports originally en-

[2] See second table.

tered into American channels of trade. The total
value of these goods then, in the hands of the initial
producers was $21,700,000,000, but before these raw
materials and goods reached ultimate consumers, they
were turned over ten times with an aggregate sales
along the line amounting to $218,599,000,000. The
final economic value of the goods, or the price paid
for them by the consumer was $65,632,000,000. In
this building up from an initial value of $21,700,-
000,000 to a final price to the consumer of $65,632,-
000,000, *processing* and *manufacturing* added a cost
of $22,500,000,000, intermediary trade added a cost
of $7,100,000,000, retailers added a cost of $12,200,-
000,000. The goods went round and round and back
and forth again and this required *transportation*
which added a cost of $8,800,000,000." [3]

We may wish to be conservative and not jump to con-
clusions from figures such as I have quoted. But should
we not recognize that great wealth does flow from the
land and does support businesses that by their nature
cannot be concerned with the grave need of rural rehabilitation?

"The goods went round and round." . . . The phrase
is a revealing one and could be taken in a light-hearted
spirit were it not for the serious thought of what it
does to people. It is a part of the urbanizing process: It
centralizes population. It shows us in transit from the
more personally reliant and provident culture to a
seller's culture.

The saving mentioned by Mr. Lincoln is not the important factor. Rural people through their co-operative

[3] *Rural Roads to Security,* Rev. G. Ligutti and J. Rawe, p. 280.

stores can build into the present-day business structure and can set up there a bridgehead of agrarian economic and social thought. That is the significance of a brood of consumer co-operatives in any given rural region. Even though they comprised only 25 per cent of the business volume of the region they could be a most powerful defender of decentralist living and rural institutions.

The achievements of the co-operatives in the United States grow more impressive year by year. There are 2,000,000 consumers in this country who own a $600,-000,000-a-year business. They own and control that business. The Co-operative League of the U. S. A., 167 West 12th Street, New York City, recently reviewed the growth of the past two years. Its news release pointed to the erection of a dozen refineries, mills and factories; the establishment of a co-operative bank; extension of electric power to nearly two hundred thousand families; modernization of co-op food stores and pioneering in the introduction of government ABC grade labeling. These developments were paralleled by similar progress in co-operative insurance, medical care, education, burial associations and student co-operatives.

It is too late to say that it can't be done. It is being done. The co-operatives, taken all together, constitute an evolving organism, which defends ownership, strengthens the hand of the common man, and has impounded as a reality within it many of the substances of democracy. It is corporate; it is at the same time democratic.

It may be optimistic to look forward to a consumer development that would team with a true agrarianism. But here I think we face one of the crucial questions of the co-operative estates. Either they become positive and teach an agrarian outlook; or they remain centralist and proletarian in the groove of the urban structure, in which case they run the risk of becoming, unwillingly and unwittingly, one of the tails of the comet which we call statism. A farmer-consumer development, taking care of the merchandising needs of people who use land and organic sources as the base of family requirements, can become a powerful agent working for the better life for more people in the country. This becomes clear to anyone who, examining the consumer set-up that is representative also of the viewpoint of the small primary producer, compares it with the privately owned farm implement, fertilizer, motor, or milling industries.

Perhaps it is not far-fetched to look forward to regional, agrarian consumer estates that will take care of much of the mass-production needs of a majority of the people who will live on land and who produce, locally and in their households, what is reasonable. When rural people own the institutions that service them in the cities, that will help decentralize wealth, work and population.

A fair price for what the tiller must buy, a fair price for what he must sell! Without these the whole rural economic structure is set on shifting sands. These it is the office of the co-operative store to help to provide. It is this producer-consumer collaboration that is held largely responsible for the spread of rural ownership in the Scandinavian countries. Where consumer organizations are being built with this outlook we may expect better things.

The agrarian movement is not merely a thing of the country. The agrarian movement has also to be built from the city outwards. Some of our labor friends have come to realize that the roots of the labor problem are in rural life. Rural youth, finding home conditions unsatisfactory, flock into towns and increase unemployment and proletarianism. But it is also correct to say that some roots of the rural problem are in the city. The drawing-in process is what the city lives upon; its pride nourished by the very numbers which kill it, its culture tends to become a negation of those universal values which rural diversity exemplifies. It cramps and restricts life.

In promoting rural life we are not talking of city people going back to the land. But there are many rural-born people in cities who would live on the land if conditions were more encouraging and if the life were seen fully in its vital reflexes. City people could do a great job for rural life without moving out of the block. They can build consumer co-operatives that become one wing of the farm economy, and a protagonist of rural causes. They thus serve the city in the best possible way. The best deal for the city is that the man on the land is content and passably prosperous. The industrial worker who builds co-operatives which help to check the exploitation that brings down rural enterprise and brings in a bankrupt labor surplus competing for his job, is doing as sensible a thing as joining and supporting a labor union. Here and there labor is becoming conscious of this large-scale nullification of its aim and effort; labor for its own integrity must soon come out on the agrarian side.

About seven years ago some men in Sydney, Nova Scotia, were becoming interested in co-operatives. The record of societies in this industrial city of 35,000 people had not been too bright. But that was before the study-club method to adult learning had been systematically conducted. Unemployment was rife. Some of the men held meetings in an old barn. They talked, too, in barber shops and kitchens about co-operatives. They joined study clubs, heard lectures and received literature and books on the topic. After some time they set up buying-clubs to buy groceries. There were many discouragements and at times they were tempted to let things go. But the thing was kept going, as a considerable adult educational program was being carried on in the field at the time.

By the summer of 1936 quite a co-operative school of thought had evolved, and on August 6 the Sydney Co-operative opened a store at Ashby Corner. Just recently —three and one-half years later—the Sydney Co-operative Society Limited, reported 900 members and the record of their growth as follows:

Period	Membership	Sales Volume
1st Six Months	259	$ 36,000.00
2nd Six Months	351	52,000.00
3rd Six Months	476	75,000.00
4th Six Months	565	100,000.00
5th Six Months	676	109,000.00
6th Six Months	805	132,000.00
7th Six Months	899	146,000.00

Total Sales $650,000.00

In this three and one-half year period, they returned to their members $42,000 and put aside reserves of $15,000. They had two branch stores and a service station in operation—the sales of the latter totaling $27,011.45 and not included in the above. When they look back, some of the members wonder at the nerve it took to tackle certain of the problems that came up.

The success of this society stimulated others. Cooperative stores were being formed in rural Cape Breton, a region of which Sydney is the business center. Older rural societies took on a new growth. A local wholesale has now been formed as an affiliate of the Maritime Central. (The headquarters of this latter body is at Moncton, New Brunswick, and will be known as the Maritime Co-operative Services or as M. C. S.) This local wholesale is now the nerve-center of forty-five societies in the region—mostly stores. The region is divided into zones. Each zone sends directors to a monthly meeting with the wholesale. They all sit down together, and the economic conditions of the region, especially as having to do with purchase and sale, come up for review. Certainly not all problems are being solved. But this, I believe, is true: the people in touch with the co-operative societies are learning more about the economics of their occupations than they ever had a chance of doing before.

Recently I attended one of these meetings. For ten hours we sat with about fifty members of this advisory council of the local wholesale in the board room of the Sydney co-operative store. Farmers, fishermen and city industrial workers discussed their joint problems as consumers. As the wholesale buys rural produce for its member-stores, farm marketing and production is one of its main interests. The marketing of fish, vegetables, poultry, lambs, timber, the matters of trucking-service and deliveries came in for close attention. Growth was demanding a new warehouse. The credit and financial standing of each one of the locals came in for an over-hauling. Credit business was condemned, and before the meeting ended it was decided that the wholesale go on a fifteen-day cash basis with its locals. Education should be paid for as a cost of co-operative business; for the purpose of educational work all societies were advised to charge one per cent on sales to operating expense. A few rural societies were weak because of bad local conditions, lack of sound production programs and non-use by the people of materials about them. Government experts gave talks on production, grading and marketing.

The representatives of the rural societies who attend these monthly meetings can take back to their neighbors a fund of knowledge. Of course, there are many difficulties to be overcome. But there is much in this that is of better promise than the old way of small farmers—going from door to door in the towns with their chickens or their turnips.

The thing to note about this is that the wholesale came into being for the most part as a result of the rise of co-operative stores in the towns. The fast-growing Sydney co-operative store has been the mainstay. In other words, there is here the start of a constructive agrarian stimulus growing from the towns outwards. It is rather soon yet to judge. But it is not far-fetched to say that future decades should show a new deal for the countryside, particularly if this economic arm can be flanked with the moral conviction that rural life is the good life for a majority and that we people of this region can really create a rural culture. If the consumer movement throughout this continent became agrarian in its emphasis, it could be a great ruralizing and de-centralizing force.

Industrial workers in Cape Breton are in a few cases becoming land-conscious. Only recently a group at Reserve Mines, in contact with stimulating co-operative thought, made representations to the Nova Scotia Government. They had been inspired by what co-operative home-building had done at Tompkinsville; without minimizing the difficulties, they are now examining the idea of carrying out a somewhat similar project, but under wholly rural conditions. Their memorandum said, in part:

"There are ten members in our Land Settlement Club. We have been meeting regularly for ten months. All of the group are married men except one. The women are interested in going on the land. Six men out of the ten were born on farms. All of the others have had experience in farming; all are now working the land in some degree, in addition to carrying on their jobs.

"We are aware of the failures in placing industrial workers on the land in the past. We believe that we understand at least some of the reasons for these failures. It is necessary that whoever goes should have a thorough philosophy of rural living. Accordingly, we have been trying to state to each other the advantages of the rural way of life undertaken by a group of seasoned co-workers—not a lonesome individual and his wife set down on a lonely farm among strange conditions of work and living. In this we have been aided by some of the best books and literature on the topic.

"We are also aware of the increasing disadvantages in making a living by working in industry. Mining is a wasting asset. Our view is that the time has come to try some new type of rural community, and we believe that if a group could go and make a success of it that others would follow.

"Our study work has been carried on, among other things, for the purpose of weeding out persons who would look upon the move as a passing whim. Before taking any definite step we want a tried and well-selected group."

One of the members of this study club wrote a letter to a government official in which he said:

"Our study group have for the past year really tried to find out what 'the land' should mean and we have come to the conclusion that it should be made the basis for a philosophy of life whereby one would be enabled to do, in this world, things that would be stepping-stones to culture and happiness and a thorough preparation for the world to come."

Several of the members of this study club have been active supporters of the Reserve Mines co-operative store and credit union for some years. And it is through businesses like these with a social outlook that their agrarian thinking has had a chance to develop. The development of true agrarian thought is necessary before action is taken. The attempts made in the past to spring jobless men out onto farms, men who were still wage-workers at heart and had no intention of being anything else, hurt the landward cause. We must first get numbers of picked men and women to go rural through moral conviction. They must be capable of diagnosing the evils that swarm in the wake of centralism. No amount of money subsidizing can produce this conviction.

But the conviction and the school of thought are not enough. Such have existed in some countries and without much fruit. In England, for instance, the conviction has lived on, at times hardly more than a literary topic, from Goldsmith to Ruskin to the Distributists of the present day. There was no economic force adequate to give reality to the ideal. The spirit was willing, but the flesh was not there. The cityward stampede has been strong enough to override all ideological obstacles.

What is needed is a strong, free economic power operating in the urban centers as well as in the country. Then the school of thought could have a body. Under certain conditions the consumer establishment offers possibilities. The consumer establishment should stand like a mountain in the economy and make cause on all fronts for rurality and decentralism.

In Canada our industrial output in 1937 was up again to what it had been in 1929, but it took 1,500,000 fewer men.

A short time ago Raymond McGowan wrote in the Providence *Visitor:*

"I have driven through parts of Louisiana, taken a train trip to San Antonio and another train trip up to the cotton country around Taylor, Texas, driven northwest up to the oil country around Wichita Falls, then into Oklahoma and across Oklahoma by way of its capital into Arkansas, across most of Arkansas, and then taken a train again up toward Chicago by way of St. Louis.

". . . A billion people would be some seven times as many people as we have at present. It seems to me now that far more than a billion people could support themselves here. The guess of two weeks ago seems timid.

". . . You ride for miles on miles and see few towns and even few farm homes. You ride through green fields. The country is rich. But it supports far too few people. Far too few people work it and far too few people live from working it. Something is terribly wrong. Something is terribly wrong and it is not the American soil, or the American sun, rain and snow. . . .

". . . 'Back to the Farm' propaganda isn't enough. I suspect an over-hauling of most of our institutions and practices, rural and urban, will be necessary to end this tragic waste of things and people."

Over-hauling of our institutions and practices, rural and urban, is a phrase that suggests action.

Obviously the drive in the ruralizing process must be something greater than the mere parochial economics or the good wishes of one-track capitalist business. Unless there is a powerful economic body, regional and autonomous, making cause for rural life, what powers of state may yet have to be invoked to establish some sane relationship between population and living space!

And it may be questioned, in the opinion of this writer at least, if producer co-operatives can do it. Have not great producer federations existed, for instance, in western Canada and in California coincident with some decline in rural life? It would seem that the man who merely sells inevitably becomes subjugated to the ideals of his market. The market has been urban. As a matter of fact simon-pure consumer advocates have always looked upon the lone producer set-up as vulnerable to pure capitalist influence. And this thread of thought that is within the consumer movement, were it integrated with a true agrarianism, would be an indisputable asset.

Workers who have followed economic reforms by means of the state and along the line that it is possible to get something for nothing have seen in Europe their theories harden first into tyrannies and then detonate into war. There is one big theory left untried. It is this: build for a rural and decentralist culture. It is something that can be done by common citizens who know instinctively that there is greatness in simple things. Let us not wait for the superman on this continent. On the asphalt the proletarian cannot loose his chains. On the nearest forty acres he might cast them off.

CHAPTER VIII

Adult Education in the Rural Community

THE accepted standards of a period produce a citizen-type. The vogue puts its mark upon the person. During the industrial expansion period the making of money has prevailed as the success ideal. The examples of success held up before young men seeking an education were mainly those who had "made good," who had made a million dollars. No one could have any right to complain of another making money as long as it did not visibly react against the common good. But whether or not fortune-building was reacting favorably or unfavorably upon the chances of average men to make a living was not always evident without study and social education; and because we have lacked a sufficiently revealing brand of social education we are in the plight that we are in today.

Dr. J. J. Tompkins says: "Do not educate any more the type of man who, after college, will want to go out and make a million. We must educate men to see the social effects of their economic activities. Educate men who will build men and go out and help in the building of co-operatives."

Up to now it has been quite natural for numbers of educated young men to plan on going into business for themselves, rather than on seeking that work which would give them an honest livelihood while at the same time they helped the condition of the community. It seems true that this imperception of the shallowness in our aims is more responsible for poverty and the present inequalities than is greed. The ease with which wealth can be gathered and kept by a fortunate few is due also to the backwardness of the people themselves.

Last winter, it was reported by the Associated Press from Washington, D. C., that the president of a certain large soap company had received $469,713 as his share of the year's business. Now, it is easy to suggest ill-will against those who receive so large an income. Such persons are not wholly to blame. Any man who can convince people that he is worth that much unquestionably must have points. The real culprit is the user of soap; and the real case for censure is against the consumers. The rancor commonly associated with such situations should be rightly directed against the lethargy, the disunity, and bone-headedness of the people themselves.

It is cases such as these, multiplied endlessly throughout the set-up of liberal capitalism, that show to the people their lost opportunities—and that underscore the importance of the consumer societies. It is the sin of omission, on the part of the people and of those who guide them, that causes the conditions which invite the acquirer to do just about as he wills with the wealth that flows from the many faucets of the business life.

Hence, it is not true that we have come to our present plight by the greed of others. We have come to our present plight by our own lethargy as well as by others' greed. The replacing of that lethargy with a spark of zeal and social creativeness is the way out of our current confusion. This can be nothing other than a warning of the spirit. The time is perhaps past to put the blame on the rich. In the words of Winston Churchill to those who would look into the past with the idea of fixing the guilt for what the world faces today: "Let every man search his own heart." It is well to put aside past resentments. In former times our business leaders had no inkling that any other way was possible, and until recently there has been but little education in the socially bad effects of big business centralization.

Education can strengthen the agrarian and decentralist trend by showing the emptiness of the modern success ideal. Under the war conditions, in which it seems probable that we shall have to live, the service motive comes in for high emphasis. Occupations that keep people solvent and self-reliant in small communities are obviously of service to the state.

One of the other things that we shall have to rid ourselves of is the worship of bigness. The big city considers itself superior to the small city; the small city considers itself superior to the town. Numbers of people become victims of quite illogical prejudices—drawing solace from the size of the crowd among whom they mill. This lack of respect for the qualities that are in small things, and this lack of the knowledge that the simple can reflect the truly great, are of the same dark genre as the revolutionary and unlimited use of force for the domination of weaker peoples and nations. Worship of bigness *is* worship of force. It is of the mob; and the mind of the mob is a cave of the winds.

Perhaps the most hopeful thing on the rural horizon is that educated men are beginning to turn landward. This is happening here and there. More men of ability

are seeing this as economic reform brought down out
of the air onto solid ground.

A short time ago I met a man who travels as a salesman for six months of the year. Until four years ago he
had lived in a city all his life. His studies during the
depression had brought him to the conviction that the
only thing that now mattered, for the good of his young
family and himself, was to get on a farm and build up a
productive rural home to the maximum. He is able to
do this and carry on his part-time salesmanship.

There are considerable numbers of men in the towns
who are getting this same idea and who are in the same
class. Part-time subsistence farming offers a new security
to them. Technology is coming to their aid: and it is
possible that there will be a steady flow of creative
energy into building the decentralist home. Paved
roads, bus service, electric power and telephone—these
suggest that the time is here for a partnership of human-
scale technology with the biological bases of land. Land
use and the self-providing family household using crafts
and simplified machinery offer certain advantages to
low-salaried workers. Home-building on the land—without becoming lyrical about the aroma of new-mown
hay—does offer play for originality and adventure. It
may be that the people who are starting to do this
constitute the vanguard of a new vogue that has promise
in relaxing economic stress in the cities. But before
the outward movement can come to its best fruition it
is necessary that those going landward become conscious
of their work on land as an integral part of an important
social reform, of, in fact, their role as soldiers in a
counter-revolution to the Industrial Revolution. They

would have to become articulate; every community of such pioneers should form an alliance of ideas with others who are doing the same thing. This can probably be done only by some adult-education set-up and by an effort in journalism. The latter is necessary even though there is only a small paper, because then there is some chance of its becoming a stimulant of redemptive social attitudes and outlook. Such a paper has to be able to live at fighting weight. A large paper is costly and usually has to make alliances which necessarily weaken its advocacy of what the people need. The set-up which I am roughly indicating is possible only in collaboration with an aggressive regional co-operative movement.

This type of educational work will be necessary because the landward movement will be contested. It will be contested, perhaps not openly, but by gentle sprayings of ridicule. If real estate values in the towns show even a slight decline in values, the Sunday supplements will discover that land has a corrupting influence on man, that life outside the city walls is morally, socially and hygienically impossible. No man, it will be intimated, in this age of conveniences can be expected to go to the hardship of plucking his own cucumbers. Land-settlement projects, falling short of Utopian success in five years, will be scrutinized and on them will be thrown the shadow of failure—when every farmer knows that it takes about a generation to create the ideal farm home. Rural environment will be interpreted as nothing more than the tinkle of a cow-bell and the crowing of a cockerel. It is all very simple. Take the spirit out of people for land and *land is a failure.* By these ways are men fooled, weakened, cheated and prepared for the conqueror.

In the co-operative movement there are four factors which make growth possible:

1. The organizers: the living word, and the discussion circles.
2. Favorable leadership, such as the clergymen, in the local community.
3. Businessmen—managers of stores, etc., who know Co-operation and have a social vision.
4. A journalism that is able to interpret Co-operation in terms of human values and to defend the movement in all fields.

Factors 1, 2 and 4 are capable of being used in the rural cause. The re-discovery of land, so to speak, by teachers, educators and editors, is one of the hopeful signs. When they live on farms themselves, even though part time, their example becomes strong. Their weight is on the side of rural living. Nothing dramatizes a value so much as to live it. And in this case we are dealing with values upon which hang the liberties of a majority of common men.

Education is the propaganda of truth; if it is not that, it is a sort of organized way to dissolve the human mind—a concealed bolshevism. The new rural adult-education will have to know all the legitimate instruments for its cause. Isolated individuals going on farms here and there, as did miners in Nova Scotia ten years ago, are foredoomed to failure. Their lonely effort is hindered and annulled by the same forces that brought about the urbanization of so many of our populations. Such projects need to be mothered by a regional movement capable not only of securing practical advantages but also of injecting a vital spirit.

Some social thinkers, in stressing the evils attendant upon great over-built cities on this continent, placed their hopes upon the towns. The provincial towns, it was hoped, would become centers of an indigenous culture. The likelihood of this grows less. The town, instead of being what once it was, namely, an economic and cultural center of its region, has become an outpost of the cities a point of consignment for mass-produced goods and culture. What can be expected of the towns in the decentralist program? In spite of the good sense of most small-town people the towns present obstacles.

George Russell (AE), the Irish advocate of rural civilization, found certain Irish towns a hindrance to rural life. He wrote:

"There are two kinds of towns, the town which exists because it is a centre of production, and the town which exists because it is a centre of distribution. I have prophesied against many Irish country towns for this sin in them, that they do not produce. Towns ought to be conductors, catching the lightnings of the human mind, and distributing them all around their area. The Irish country towns only develop mental bogs about them. We have grown so accustomed to these arid patches of humanity that we accept them in a hopeless kind of way, whereas we should rage and prophesy over them as the prophets of ancient Israel did over Tyre and Sidon.

And indeed a lordly magnificence of wickedness is not so hopeless a thing to contemplate as a dead level of petty iniquity, the soul's death in life, without ideas or aspirations." [1]

A rural and provident culture cannot spring from the viewpoint of educators who remain in the ruts of town-thinking. The carriers of the new rural education will themselves live on the land. They will aid in spreading scientific agriculture. The most valuable scientist in agriculture is the man who lives on the land and who farms under conditions fairly representative of the average farmer. But scientific farming, while an important factor, cannot produce a rural culture. The knowledge tends to be picked up by a few smart men who become big farmers. The preservation of the family, ancestral and self-sufficient homes to last one hundred years, soil and race—these are motives that may enter into renewed rural life.

The idea of subsistence-farming suffers somewhat from the word *subsistence*. It is understood by some as a state of merely existing. This is somewhat unfortunate and may be grossly untrue. The lords of the manor, on their broad estates, were subsistence-farmers. The citizen who makes some money at other work may well live on a farm as a safe and healthful base of foodstuffs and other essentials. The idea of subsistence-farming is of immense significance in relation to the social problem. It means that no matter how low the income may fall from non-farm sources (job, salary, etc.) the country home is there and is sole ground for food, fuel

[1] *A Memoir of AE*, by John Eglinton, Macmillan, pp. 78, 79.

and shelter. A much more widely popularized realization of this would react against the decline of initiative which relief invites.

Low-salaried people who can save nothing when living in towns can save when they become established on a farm within commuting distance. By growing much of their food and doing some of their own work, and by providing children with conditions of gainful, character-building work at home, the difference soon becomes substantial. The participation of such people in rural occupations helps the tone of rural living.

The question is sometimes asked: What good is it for more people to be using land when farmers already lack markets? Would it not hurt the existing market for farm produce?

The answers to so general a question could only be suggested in reference to the conditions which exist in local regions. In Maritime Canada, for instance, there could be a large increase in farm production in many lines before we would supply our own urban market. But the main answer to the question is that the urgent human problem of the over-populated city cannot be solved in terms of markets alone, or in terms of utilitarian expediency alone. Also, an insecure proletariat does not provide a stable urban market. Then, too, there is the over-production in certain sections of North America in lines like wheat or cotton, and the need has become recognized for a more diversified type of agriculture. The more diversified and self-sufficient types of agriculture relieve the farmer of such close dependence upon markets.

The most serious problem in land settlement is that

of those who go on the land and must make their total
living from it. Very frequently such people have little
or no money to start with. It is hard to see how this can
be done successfully today except in co-operative communities. Just what should be held co-operatively and
what individually is something to be worked out. One
of the reasons for the decline of the old type of rural
community was that the people were too far apart. The
relation between welfare and density of population has
been ignored in the patternless settlements.

Men who have worked in mines and factories have
learned something about working in common—as a
crew. Very often such men do not become contented
workers alone, such as the individual farmer far removed from a neighbor. They have learned of the lift
that there is in numbers; five men working together are
more than five men. Our pioneer forefathers understood well this strength in social labor and by help of it
they conquered the forests of the continent.

Some people will go on land along with a group
(even 12 or 15 families which would be a nucleus of
what would later be a larger community) who would
not go otherwise. They would perhaps give a new shape
to the rural community. Houses would be close together. Certain parts of the land would be held in
common. Certain operations could, perhaps, be carried
on by the men as a co-operative group—saving in costs
of farm machinery and buildings. The allotment of
work and the division of the proceeds present difficulties. But the boon of, say, twelve carefully selected
men working daily together would be great; the psychological effects could be advantageous if the members

had the true co-operative attitudes and there was the religious leadership that could dissolve resentments. At any rate this possible new pattern deserves to be regarded with an open mind. If the associative techniques which some workers have learned in factories and labor unions can be channeled in land communities, that would be a gain. Twelve settlers working harmoniously together could perhaps in five years bring their respective homesteads up to a point which a lone settler could hardly hope to achieve in ten years. It is loneliness, and the slowness in the results of his labor, that break the morale of the individual settler.

Fellowship of the spirit makes a community. To make a community the persons have to hold communion with each other. They have to meet frequently, talk, and understand each other. The people who make up a true community will have a common outlook on the great major issues of life; the same view of man and human society and their destinies. If they are Christians, they will aim at realizing the brotherhood of man; the concept of Charity which was the making of Christianity at its origin would be such among the members that each could work for the group in full faith that each would get back from the group what justice required. The fear of insecurity, as it is known in the chaotic individualistic world, would be absent in such a community, because if a member got into difficulties he would be carried by the brotherhood, and without stigma.

Such a community could only be the outcome of a school of thought. Before it could be attempted the members would have to be schooled in certain funda-

mentals; they would have to be thoroughgoing co-
operators, and certainly not in the superficial sense of
merely climbing upon a prominent bandwagon, but
with a full awareness of all the interior disciplines and
sacrifices that go into the making of a co-operator.

In connection with a land-and-crafts economy, is it
far-fetched to consider the building of new rural communities with this new soul in them? In many existing
places, individualism intercepts the several values required. Individualism does not offer any hope for the
new castoff class—the unemployed. It does seem, then,
that the time is ripe for the kind of action suggested.

Land settlement is a challenge to adult education.
Is our brand of education made of the strong stuff that
tries to meet urgent human needs? Has it compassion
enough upon man's suffering to get humble, risk failures and stain its hands?

There is also the problem of revitalizing existing
rural communities. One of the first needs in rural adult
education will be to find the men gifted in interpreting
the rural environment, in its philosophical significance,
in its role in building the individual, the family, the
nation. We need men who, like the poets, can brood
over this land and say the truths that will make its
youth feel proud to have soil on their boots. Back of the
economics and the mere mechanics of an agrarian restoration must be a philosophy.

Horace Plunkett went to Denmark to study farming
methods and co-operation. Of him it was said that while
he had come "to investigate a piece of machinery (sic)
he remained to study a philosophy." [2] This philosophy

[2] *Denmark, A Social Laboratory*, Peter Manniche, Oxford Univ. Press.

came from the folk schools and its distinctive note was that the person should be taught just relationships with his community rather than given merely information. The young man was given time to keep in touch with the farm, and was held, at periods, to devote himself to farm work. He was guided to live and work as a member of the community. He was made conscious of the historic and spiritual values of his region and out of this emerged the *folk spirit*.

Here in North America lies ahead, as one of the big jobs, the evoking of the folk spirit. The landward and decentralist movement cannot get very far without it. We must have folk schools. These should be as informal as possible, and should spring up around men who are capable of interpreting rural values and of living the rural life. A rural life that has lost its self-respect before the pride of the cities cannot produce a culture. I believe that in the making of rural communities folk-lore and poetry will come to receive renewed importance. Folk-lore is one of the springs of community spirit. Most rural communities are unconscious of their own worth. They sent the bright sons to town. They parted with their pride and lost their souls. They forgot the greatness of the fathers. All the valor, all the pathos of men, who in the first fine raptures of freedom cleared the wilderness, built soil, and accepted hardship as the price of the dignity of independence, were lost—or shall we hope only withheld? A true folk-lore is the memory of the race. It cannot die. This epic of the fathers is part of our self-respect. It will be one of the elements in the rebirth of the local community. Local history, preserving the heroic spirit of the folk memory, is part of the moral equipment in the decentralist process. Why should not the pathos of the past pulse through the present? We need it. Industrialism had broken this continuity, but the industrial center should no longer hold first place. The rural youth needs the attitudes that will let him stay at home with pride and spirit—and with a sense of his high commission from the past, his high pledge to the future. One might ask, why is not local history, as seen by persons capable of carrying forward the valors of the past, taught in local schools?

Akin to the folk memory is poetry. The profane eye sees only the profane in the crude fathers of the village. But the poet knows the dignity of the bent back; he knows the worth and wonder of common things, and that there are meditative estates of man as well as material. The true poetic vision should help a people break through the superficial sense of values which draws them into economic slavery and fixes the main effort of their souls at keeping up with the Joneses.

CHAPTER IX

Bread and Beauty

THE Antigonish Movement is Adult Education for Action. Specifically, it is action toward righting some of the wrongs in the economic order. It is, therefore, to be distinguished from adult education, which is purely cultural in the sense of ornate. It values the truly cultural as much as does any school, but it believes in a different approach. It considers tolerable economic conditions to be an important first step toward the higher things. It does not try to put Beauty in the place of Bread, nor Bread in the place of Beauty. It believes in both. And because it believes in both, it starts with Bread.

It seems good sense to say that the place for educators —and moralists—to meet contemporary man is at the point of his chief anxiety. Individualism has brought the world to a state of high-tensioned insecurity. We need no sentimental over-emphasizing of the facts that in society today there are want, fear, the sense of frustration, the indignity of the dole. These are realities. These are the sore spots in the hearts of contemporary man.

Can education tighten its belt and do something adult about it? Or should education stay on comfortable ground? Should it lay hold of non-combatant's rights in the social struggle and perform a Red Cross activity?

So far as Antigonish is concerned, there can be no question as to its stand. The initiation of credit unions, co-operative stores, lobster factories, marketing associations and co-operative housing furnishes the answer. A marked stimulation to credit-union formation and growth, as well as to other projects of a co-operative nature, has taken place. The latest report of the Inspector of Co-operatives for Nova Scotia, an impartial source, revealed that there were 67 co-operatives in the Province. This included all types (credit unions excepted). There were 27 consumers' societies.

In Newfoundland, Co-operation made strides in the three years following its introduction by the Commission of Government. Fishermen, for example, market over 1,000,000 lbs. of live lobster co-operatively. Prince Edward Island and New Brunswick have vigorous credit-union developments, and co-operative stores are beginning to appear. All in all, the attitude towards co-operatives grows stronger, more confident throughout Canada.

I do not mean to suggest that it is easy to teach people through study clubs to build and run their own co-operative institutions. It is not. It is a hard job, going against the current, and it takes exceptional faith and persistence. The Movement so far has merely scratched the surface.

Wherever you find genuine successful co-operatives, you also find several persons who have caught the vital philosophy of the thing into their souls; and it is their vision and their dedication to it that make success. So, more important than the mere statistics of the program are the reasons behind it and the fundamental ideas that go into the making of good co-operators.

This would take us back to ideas that were the first beginnings of the Antigonish Movement—which of course were copied widely from the older movements, but had original slants of their own. I suggest a few of these—as I see them. Reservation should be made for personal interpretation. The reader may be referred to *The Future of the Antigonish Movement* and *The Techniques of Democracy,* by Dr. J. J. Tompkins and to *Masters of Their Own Destiny,* by Dr. M. M. Coady, also to papers delivered and articles written by several other men of the Antigonish group who have put their effort and thinking into the Movement.

The founders of the Movement were in intimate contact with the problems of fishermen, farmers, and industrial workers. Dr. Tompkins had been a pioneer in the people's education. It was decided in 1928 by St. Francis Xavier University to open an Extension Department. Dr. Coady, Professor of Education, made a survey of university extension work in the United States and became director of the new department. In 1930, A. B. MacDonald, B.S.A., who had been one of the first agricultural representatives in that part of the country and had expert knowledge of farm marketing problems, was added to the staff. He made a study of the extension work of Canadian universities.

The program decided upon was dictated by what were considered to be the greatest needs of the people. It did not emphasize courses in business, English or psychology; it emphasized courses in co-operation, handicrafts, or the building of credit unions. The needs of the people pointed to these. As Dr. Tompkins says, "We got ideas from the people, synthesized them, and gave them back to the people." It was the inductive approach. It soon became a program with concrete projects in the making. Though not without great difficulties, it had powerful elements of motivation. The method used was the small study club. It was inexpensive and could be extended over a wide area.

The Extension Department provides these groups with motivating and study material. An eight-page journal, the aim of which has been to inspire and uncover the reasons why people should build up their co-operative institutions, has been published twice a month since 1933. The Department also services the study clubs and all interested parties with pamphlets, mimeographed material, small traveling libraries, and maintains an open shelf library.

The need for a regional library system has become pronounced. It is being recognized that people who do not read do not become socially enlightened. They are easy victims of the exploiter. The wide diffusion of good books is essential to the building-up of the economically and politically enlightened good men in the local communities who are needed as the personnel of this evolving social movement. People who do not read are not only ignorant of how their livelihoods are abducted by the processes of centralized capitalism, but they are also incapable of conducting their own economic institutions. They lack the larger vision, and the zeal of dedication to the building of their local cell of the better social order; and envy and jealousy may soon split the ranks. Regional libraries with branches in the local communities are regarded as a necessary instrument in the program.

This inductive approach in adult education opens the door upon significant things. On the ground of

practical education, the question may be asked: Who
has the right to say you should learn this, or you should
learn that? Should a small circle of well-meaning
officials in departments of education, often considerably
removed from the welter and sweat and anxiety of the
common people, set courses and consider nothing else
worthy of the name of education? What is the source of
their mandate? What relation has their thinking with
democracy? They may say that teaching young people
how to build houses for themselves, how to farm, or
form co operatives that will give them entry into the
economic life, is not education. But if the people say
it is, and for the very good reason that it meets their
urgent need, then why isn't it education? We all con-
cede the desirability of everyone's learning to read and
write. Beyond that and still on the ground of practical
education, who is to say, "Learn this, don't learn that?"
In such a situation there is one court of appeal: the
people.

The masses may be said always to be right in some
things, because there are some things which only the
masses know. He who suffers knows. In the realm of the
practical working of economic systems, the common
man may be said to be the scientist; it is he who ex-
periences the loss and the gain that others theorize
about. He has something to offer; and even though he
himself is mute, his condition will speak for him.
Neither the planning of the bureaucrats, nor the profit-
making and so-called efficiency of individualists, can
produce a full-bodied program for the people. Planning,
special knowledge, and true efficiency all enter, but
they must be met by that vital germ—what the people

need and know to be right. The people should arise then and do the job themselves. Thus can the constructive and peaceful enthusiasm and talents of the people be evoked. This ground-swell is distinctly of the temper of democracy in its vital epochs, and, it may be said, distinctly at variance with the *status quo* and with the views of those who, while mouthing undisputed platitudes about democracy, constantly carry the inflections and humors of extractive capitalism into the field of education.

The Antigonish Movement has been saying that the people should do the job themselves. They should be guided to know a fool, or an exploiter, or an anti-social economic procedure when they see one. They should master the techniques of working together. These are essential in self-help. "We are not building co-operatives," says Dr. Tompkins, "we are building men. You must be 'fishers of men.' Primarily we are not seeking ideas. We are seeking men who have the social vision."

I have been told of the statement of a young man who has built himself a home by becoming a member of a co-operative housing group. He said: "I have learned more in the last year than I did in the other twenty-seven years of my life." It may be worth considering this man's experience and evaluating it in true human terms, if not in terms which customary education has set for itself. He did not mean that he had learned more from books or from courses on paper. He meant that he and his fellows had learned that they could really get together, that they could work together, help one another, raise money, plan—in a word, they had become co-operators. He had learned how to tap the sources of human solidarity. When you come to think it over, he did get an education that he could not get any other way.

But he has been getting more than an education in the old sense. Along with it he has been assembling the materials of living. To a degree he has achieved the union of learning and living. Is not this the vital union which the Greeks are said to have achieved, and which needs emphasis today when learning is so plentiful in the academic sense and living so scarce in the economic sense? He is getting a training in both the will and the intellect.

To become a good co-operator takes very definite schooling of the will. A man has to learn to get along with his fellows, to respect differences, to seek common ground and to work on that, to put his thinking into the good of the group, to bear criticism, to subdue jealousy. The whole experience is a school of character. It takes humility—the first step in learning. It exercises love of mankind.

As for the intellect, the scope for its development is considerable. So also is the scope for acquiring skills, as the rules require the men do as much of the work as possible themselves. The motivation is pretty nearly perfect. All the elements of learning are here. And when the young student has completed this particular project, he has the great advantage of having something substantial, in this case a home, which will help him to go on to other fields.

One melancholy comparison comes to mind here, that of the college graduate. He, too, wanted a home. But is it unusual today to find him, at thirty-five, homeless or immobile under his father's roof? I wish to make clear that I imply no slur against the training of the professions or the search of pure truth. Who would be so foolish as to argue against these? More power to the contemplative processes of the mind and all that conduces thereto. These things are contingent upon a certain freedom from economic slavery; their importance only adds to the importance of the type of education for living, alluded to above, which has been so frequently and justly described as fundamental. And both types—both Bread and Beauty—are so much a part of mankind's universal hunger that educators could seek to extend them to the rank and file and to revitalize themselves in the doing. When we consider the poverty, the demoralizing futility, the fear, the passing of the sense of responsibility with the passing of the true idea of work, and the substitution in its place of the custom of nomadic job-hunting, it seems evident that this project-education is but the resetting of education in the order of Charity. The claim of human brotherhood calls for it. We are at a juncture in history where it is imperative to push the kind of education that will aid in the saving of Liberty. This kind of education applied on a wide scale by voluntary zeal could stand over against statism.

The Antigonish Movement affirms that there must be evoked a concept of Charity—in its full meaning of love—which is of proportionate stature to the machine, scientific, and technical investiture of the age. Individualism has dated. The alms concept of Charity has dated. It is still fine to give the homeless a lodging for the night, but it is still better and more *ad rem* to hasten activity that will permit the homeless a home of his own if he so wishes. This heritage, accumulated through the ages, belongs in part to all men. This bigger heritage than past ages knew requires a bigger Charity than past ages knew. Otherwise it becomes a source of tyranny and envy. The age needs more than the alms concept of Charity; it needs more than the idea of organized Charity. It needs a creative and militant Charity, that is, Love which proclaims the dignity of even the lowest individual and works to actualize the brotherhood of man in the group forms which the technical genius of the age makes necessary. This is the kind of Charity which supplies one of the conditions of a new Christian social order. It is a condition within the person and can actuate economic institutions only insofar as it radiates from persons. But its first promptings may arise when the person gets the vision of what good he can do for his fellowman.

The Antigonish Movement believes in the person. Benefits to the person it pronounces to be the reason and justification for association of any kind. The society is the lengthened and strengthened hand of the man— the instrument by which his rights are the more effectively upheld, by which his initiatives are carried into wider fields. This divides, by an impassable gulf, our idea of association from that concept by which the higher and larger body may arrogate to itself the functions which can be properly performed by the smaller and local body. But this local autonomy, whether of the society or finally of the individual, cannot be counted on as effective to cope with social problems until local action is evoked and the people are conditioned to realize their power. Specifically, this means devising the economic patterns adequate to the job. This evoking is the work of adult education.

One of the aims of adult education for co-operation is to bring into being the economic institutions which by their spirit and their form will set up a wealth-diffusing activity. A friend of the Movement predicts what is ahead in a particular fishing and farming section which he has had under review. "We are engaged," he said, "in reversing the direction of the dole." He went on to explain that, for several generations, a few business houses and politicians have been harvesting fat fortunes from the economic processes which stem from the people. In recent years many of the poorer people had to be put on the dole. The point is that the wealthy business interests had been quietly on the dole—and a very large dole—for two or three generations. This has been the respectable and approved economic custom and no ill-will is directed at its beneficiaries. But the time has arrived when it is necessary to reverse the process and innocuously pass back to the people, who have been getting a miserable weekly allowance, their proportionate share of whatever business is being carried on. In this way, it is hoped the dole in all its demoralizing forms may be in time eliminated. The people are being inspired through study clubs to form co-operatives.

To the Antigonish associates, it seems that centralism has reached its acme, has gone past it, and overflowed into unemployment. There is needed a relocalization of initiatives and culture. We hope to be laying the groundwork for a reinvigorated rural life that will be a reintegration of the good things of town and country. Critics have said that this fret about the practical is a dismaying phenomenon in education. "What shall become of the higher things?" they ask.

Bread to the hungry is a high thing. Bread lays the foundation for Beauty. Nay, the getting of Bread, to be justly divided among men, is also the making of Beauty.

NOTE: This chapter was prepared for the Educational Yearbook 1940, which deals with problems of Adult Education in 16 countries (Teachers College, Columbia University, I. L. Kendel, Ph.D., Editor).

CHAPTER X

Folks Talk Shop

The job of building the co-operative estates of the people is brought to our own doors by the co-operative store.

A number of average people in a sample community —let us call it Folkdale—have become interested and have formed a discussion circle. One of the group acts as leader. There are some ten members in the group and they meet once a week. In between time they read co-operative periodicals and pamphlets and talk a good deal. They are trying to get a thorough grasp of Rochdale principles—after which they may start a store of their own.

Their talk takes them across economic ground which the majority of people can recognize as their own. Here in the very briefest outline is the substance of their dialogues.

Meeting No. 1

*Topic: The First Rochdale Principle—One Man,
One Vote*

Leader: Most poor people who work hard every day for a living will agree that an attack on poverty is long overdue. They know that technically this is an age of plenty if people did the right thing by each other.

They know, too, in a vague way that there exist today big cartels and monopolies whose owners have made huge fortunes dealing in the everyday necessities of workpeople, and have become as a consequence powerful in the political life of the country. This we all realize. But we do not always realize that we are the cause of it. Our pennies, vagrant and spent without thought, make the monopolies. The rich man is the child of our apathy. Perhaps the abuse of wealth is in part due to us and we are somewhat guilty. What do you think?

Henry: There is one way by which the people can help to remedy this condition. It is by putting their spending power together and setting up a co-operative store to be conducted along time-proven principles. Something has been said about that at the past meetings.

Peter: What are those principles?

Leader: There are seven important principles, though some students have it differently. Let me read them. 1. One man, one vote. 2. Low, fixed rate of interest on capital. 3. All business shall be done for cash. 4. Goods shall be sold at the market price. 5. Over and above operating costs and provision for education, the earnings of the business shall be rebated to the membership in the form of patronage dividends. 6. The society shall observe political and religious neutrality. 7. Reserves shall be set aside and provision made for education.

Peter: Taking that first principle—one man, one vote —how does it work out?

Henry: The money to run a co-operative store is raised by selling shares to the members. This first principle means that, no matter how many shares a member may take out, he will have only one vote in any of the affairs of the society which come before the membership.

Isadore: What is so wonderful about that?

Leader: It may seem trivial but it is very important. It makes it impossible for any person, no matter how well-to-do, to gain undue influence in the business.

Peter: Do all societies observe it?

Henry: All bona fide co-operatives observe strictly this rule, I'm told. In fact, if they don't they soon cease to be co-operatives. If the rule is not followed, a member who is able to buy several shares may so dominate that the business comes more and more under his hand. Soon all the other Rochdale principles are ignored and the business becomes the property of an individual instead of the property of a group.

Mrs. MacDaniel: It means then, that should I take out six shares in our store, at, say $5.00 per share, I will have no more to say than my neighbor who will take one?

Leader: That's it exactly, madam.

Isadore: Doesn't this rule amount to saying that any blockhead who takes the notion to join and has the price of a share will have as much to do with running the society as a man who knows business?

Henry: First of all, the society is run by the board of directors and the manager, though final authority is always vested in the general membership. But, of course, not all questions come before the general membership. In questions that do come before that body, say at the annual meeting, there can always be enough intelligent persons to out-vote blockheads.

Mrs. MacDaniel: It seems to me that if more of the men took part in co-operative projects from youth, there would not be so many blockheads, as you call them. In rural communities especially there are often sterling characters who do not get a chance to develop themselves.

Peter: I can see where there is a great truth in this principle that we are talking about. One man, one vote. Money not even mentioned. Yet it is business we're talking about. It doesn't seem like it. Hasn't the system that we've always known maintained that only money counts? Money talks, it said! And isn't that what's wrong with the world and keeps the poor, poor? Well, here's an idea that puts the person before the dollar. I'm for it. It looks human.

Leader: The time has passed very quickly. I can see that this is going to be an interesting way to study our problems here in this community. Now you folks may wish to talk on further here or at your homes, and do some reading. At our next meeting we will take up the second great Rochdale principle.

MEETING No. 2

Topic: The Second Rochdale Principle—Fixed Rate of Interest on Capital

Leader: Here we are again! I presume you members have done some reading on the Rochdale principles. These are considered, as you know, all-important rules in running a co-operative store. For nearly one hundred years they have been tested and proven right. One gathers that these principles are coming to receive more emphasis in our whole economic life. Only a short time ago, I read that a religious organization in the United States affirmed that the Rochdale principles introduced Christian attitudes into economics. We should all know them thoroughly, as we are likely to hear more and more of them in years to come. At our meeting last week we threshed out the first—one man, one vote. This evening we tackle the second. It reads: That interest paid on capital be at a low, fixed rate. Now, I'm sure you other members have something to say.

Isadore: It's all very well to talk about Christian attitudes on paper. But at the pay-off the small producer gets skinned. Look at how I was treated with my smelts last season! Just when I had a good catch the bottom fell out of the market. I hardly more than broke even. It's a marketing system we want, not a store, I'd say.

Henry: How are you going to get a marketing system?

Peter: That is the point. Perhaps perfect control of the many market conditions is out of the question. But this I do believe—the people who have the most control over the market are the people who are in business. And the way small producers can get a foothold in business is through the co-operative store.

Mrs. MacDaniel: To me it is very clear. The store is the right step. To sell well, it is also necessary to buy well. And as we have not always to sell, but have constantly to buy some things, the store is our way of entering the business world in the long run.

Leader: Well, anyway let us return to this second Rochdale principle. The fact that interest on shares is fixed and stationary gives stability to business. One big thing, I'm told, is that it cuts out speculation in the stocks of co-operatives.

Peter: That makes the co-operative set-up different from the capitalistic set-up—where interest on stocks goes up or down according to profits.

A Member: When that happens, as in corporations, there is trading in stocks. I have read of the dishonest practices that arise—speculation, over-capitalization, watered stock. A great deal of this actually exists in big business, as is proven by several government investigations.

Leader: I think the member has touched on a very big evil. I am not an expert on this. But I can see that when the profits of a business are distributed in the form of higher interest on the capital and on that alone, it tends to help those who have the most capital, that is, those who need help least. Also, in periods of prosperity, too much capital is drawn into such a set-up, much more capital frequently than is needed to run the business.

Isadore: Why should the stockholders of such a company let in more capital than is needed and pay interest on it?

Henry: This is done to keep the profits from looking too great. More stock is issued instead of passing the earnings back to consumers or wage-earners.

Peter: Take, for instance, the case of Big Town Light and Power. Original shares worth $100 had grown in thirty years to be worth $1,140, according to statements made in *Hansard,* March 1, 1934. I have some more figures here in my notebook. What about the price of electricity to the consumer, you might ask? Well, I quote from the *Big Town News,* December, 1924: "The rates per K.H. have been 1,200% higher than the rates in Ottawa." And all because the earnings of the business went to capital.

Mrs. MacDaniel: That is a very respectable form of dishonesty, if I may put it that way. Multiply such a trend through the great corporations and you see at work a merciless formula of pauperization. Usury was forbidden in certain ages by the moral authorities. Those grand Rochdale pioneers were very far-seeing.

Isadore: Just the same, if I get only a low, fixed interest on shares why should I invest at all?

Members: You will learn that as you go along. There are some good sound reasons.

Leader: The discussion has brought home to us points that we can all appreciate. The question is: Are we going to follow through and do something about it? You may wish to continue this discussion. At our next meeting we will take up the third Rochdale principle: Business shall be done for cash.

MEETING No. 3

Topic: The Third Rochdale Principle—Goods Shall Be Sold for Cash

Leader: In our circle this evening we take up what, I am told, is a most important rule of co-operative business. I assume you other members have been reading up on it. It says that all business at a co-op store should be done for cash. This seems to be a strange voice in the land—this cash business. Most everyone has been telling us that instalment buying is just the thing. "A dollar down and a dollar a week," "Easy terms," "Your credit is good with us," etc.—these have been the rallying cries in the marketplace.

Mrs. MacDaniel: Yes. It takes a quite strong character to go shopping in safety in most towns, or to read the mail-order catalogues, or even the ad sections of magazines! So many wants are aroused! So much easy credit! It is as if a day of reckoning would never come. One has to be cruel with oneself in order to stay solvent. I know!

Henry: In such a system of pushing goods upon the public there is never any indication given that credit costs—and costs dearly. If we people only stopped to figure—

Peter: I was reading on that point only last evening after supper. My wife had me make a note of it. It says that Dr. J. G. Knapp, of the Farm Credit Administration, Washington, made a study of this question. He made a credit survey of fifty-eight oil and gas co-ops in the United States. He found that credit was costing them fourteen per cent of their overhead.

Leader: Well, now, that is amazing. And who do you suppose pays for this extra?

Two Members: The cash customer pays.

Isadore: Then why be a cash customer? When you have to pay for the other fellow too! Me, I think it's pretty handy to be able to run up a bill at a store. Now, I see it really pays—

Peter: Oh, don't worry! In such a case you get hooked too. The cost of credit is really borne by all the customers—the credit ones as well as the cash ones.

Henry: It raises the cost of running the business,

which in turn is reflected in prices and the earnings of the business.

Leader: I think perhaps Isadore brought out a point he didn't mean to. He said in effect, why be a cash customer if you have to help carry the credit customers. It is said that once you start giving credit you can't stop it. Everyone wants it. Pretty soon everyone is getting credit and there is no cash customer. The store will get bogged down. The remedy is to give no credit at all. The men of Rochdale and their followers insisted on that.

Isadore: I like credit anyhow. This cash business may be all right in theory, but theory never puts tobacco in my pouch.

Henry: Take now the case of your smelts there, Isadore. Last meeting you were talking about the trouble you had to sell them at a reasonable profit. Don't you think that if the people owned stores they would have the greatest possible agency to ensure that the small primary producers got fair prices? They would also buy more cheaply the things that go into production. They would have wholesales. And here is my point: such a system can't be built on credit.

Isadore: I had not thought that far into it. It's pretty far-fetched. But if it could be made to come true—

Mrs. MacDaniel: It will take time. But the years pass swiftly. A co-operative is a step that can be taken by ourselves at once. What if our fathers had done this fifty years ago? Things today would not be perfect, it is true, but I think there would be in existence a great force in favor of the average poor man.

Leader: Yes. Provided the Rochdale principles were

followed, and especially this one of doing business for cash, I can see great advantages. Without the cash business the stores do not get far. With credit, the manager is handicapped in buying the goods from the wholesale. The wholesale, in turn, is hampered and kept from going into production and putting in facilities and new lines. Credit permits, at best, a puny movement which dies. Now, I see that our time is up.

Several Members: Already? Why, there are several more questions on this principle. Can we take it up again at next meeting?

MEETING No. 4

Topic: The Third Rochdale Principle—Goods Shall Be Sold for Cash

Leader: We are still discussing the rule of cash business as applied in co-operative stores. At our last meeting we studied it. Several members, in fact I think all of us, were of the opinion that there is a great deal to know about this rule and that it is a most important one. We saw that any store giving credit thereby raises its overhead fourteen per cent. We saw how giving credit to the customer weakens the society, weakens the wholesale works all down through the movement, causing it to be stunted and, perhaps, in time to die. When the societies do not have enough cash business to do a cash business with the wholesale, the latter cannot provide the facilities—buildings, warehouses, expert staff, etc.—of entry into new lines which would mean great savings to the consumer-members. On this we agree, do we not?

Peter: Yes. The history of co-operation shows that beyond all doubt. In the case of mass-produced, manufactured goods, there is always a sharp lowering of prices when consumers through their stores reach what is called the point of production. For example, fertilizer has fallen $3.00 per ton in Ohio. The reason? The co-op wholesale had eighteen months back gotten hold of certain fertilizer plants.

Mrs. MacDaniel: That is quite a change. It is going up in the Maritimes—though I understand we had already gotten the advantages of pooled fertilizer buying some years back. But I think it shows how building a strong consumer set-up is the sure way to a better deal for the producer.

Henry: And that means cash business! Not only does the small producer get a lower price on the things he has to buy, but there are also being set up for him the facilities of a marketing system.

A Member: That is right. A man who joins a co-op store with the intention of buying on credit and running up bills is putting his head into a bag.

Isadore: Bag or no bag, when you're broke it's handy to be able to get what you need on credit. This business of lowering the price of fertilizer is great. And setting up market outlets for what we farmers and fishermen have to sell—that's great, too. But that takes time. In the meantime we are, many of us, short of ready money.

Several Members: There is the credit union. The credit union! By putting aside a very small amount regularly you can soon build up an agency of your own that will take care of your ordinary loans, and whose business it is to service these loans. So you should not absolutely have to run bills at the store.

Isadore: How can you put it aside if you haven't got it? *(aside to member)* Can you give me a match? This tobacco is hard to keep lit, must be green.

Mrs. MacDaniel: But does it take so much? Now, it seems to me that for 25 cents a week it can be worked. That is $1.00 a month—$12.00 a year. If done regularly one is in good standing in the credit union. And if one shows character and is industrious most loans that otherwise would be on the books at the store as credit could be handled this way.

Henry: How much do we spend on tobacco, Isadore, in a week? I smoke three large packs of cigarettes. That is seventy-five cents.

Isadore: Well, what with this pipe—puff! puff! a few cigarettes, and some chewing, it runs, oh! not more than sixty cents a week.

Members: And it all goes up in smoke. It all goes up in smoke.

Mrs. MacDaniel: You can build a very great co-operative movement on what goes up in smoke. You've read of the great tobacco fortunes in the United States. That heiress! What's her name? Has one of the largest fortunes. It was made by you sixty-cents-a-week men. . . .

Peter: At church on Sunday I heard a sermon on the theme of gathering up the crumbs. The preacher was talking credit unions. I shall never forget it. If we add up what we spend on tobacco, what we spend on beer, and various other foolishness, and put one-third of it in our co-ops we would soon have establishments able to defend the rights of the people. A lot of poverty is our own fault.

Leader: Our time is getting short. I think it is clear to everyone that we can get away from credit if we really want to, that credit cripples Co-operation, and that when our store opens here in Folkdale it will be on a cash basis.

At our next meeting we will take up the fourth Rochdale principle: Goods shall be sold at the market price.

MEETING No. 5

Topic: The Fourth Rochdale Principle—Goods Shall Be Sold at the Market Price

Leader: It seems quite fitting that we are holding this meeting here in the kitchen of our good neighbor Peter White. The topic of discussion is that things bought at the co-op store are to be paid for at the market price. And it seems quite proper to be talking about prices in the kitchen where the need for so many of our everyday necessities originates.

Peter: My wife, alas, can originate needs in every room of this house, I've found.

Mrs. White: This is the first time that I've ever been at a study club. It sounds most interesting. I want to hear a little more before I can feel sure that I can hold my own—

Isadore: I see by the papers that there's a cut-price sale on at this new chain store in town. It looks good to me. A fellow can save a good many pennies by watching for those bargains as they come along.

Henry: That's the very point we are considering. This cut-price business is like throwing a smelt to catch a salmon. You can get a bargain on Saturdays maybe in a pair of socks or a cheap shirt. But if you are dealing for your full needs you'll pay it back. The "loss-leaders" are just bait. Besides you can never get to own the business, and that is the all-important thing; because when you own the business you have an instrument to defend your other economic, political and social rights.

Mrs. MacDaniel: Two men at Sydney, Nova Scotia, recently decided to give a test order to one of the cut-price stores; they sent exactly the same order to the co-operative. It comprised about twenty-six items. Counting a six per cent dividend the total charge at the co-op left the buyer eleven cents to the good. The quality of the goods was very much in favor of the co-op. So was the service. Not to mention the point that Henry just explained—the building up of ownership by the people through patronizing their own store.

Leader: I understand that in the early days of Co-operation in England the cost-plus method of running a store was tried. They lowered prices, charging just enough to pay the costs and overhead. It was not a success. The stores all failed in time. Underselling the other stores caused a great deal of ill-will. A fatal mistake. There were no earnings to put into the wholesale —an end to which all stores should build. Thus, a strong movement that could really bring the benefits of Co-operation to the people was nipped in the bud. The Rochdale pioneers changed this. They made it the rule to sell at the market price and rebate earnings above reserves, funds for education and investment in wholesale facilities. It has proven its worth and is largely responsible for the solid development of Rochdale societies in many countries.

Peter: As I see it, it is not going to matter what prices we pay at our store when we get it started. So long as it is efficiently run! Anything that might be over, comes back in rebates or goes into expansion which in turn brings us benefits. We will be paying a manager and know that we are not contributing to the profits of chains and absentee capitalists.

A Member: There is one question I would like to ask. If a store sells at the market price, does it have to buy at the market price? I am thinking of goods produced by sweatshop methods. Or of farm produce that has often been put on the market at prices ruinous to the farmer. It seems to me that co-op stores should do nothing that would cause such injustices to continue.

Leader: Co-op stores in the Maritimes stand for the just price—to the producer and to the consumer. They can in some cases give a better price to the farmer without raising the price to the consumer. They do this by eliminating middlemen's profits. As they get stronger it is easier for them to agree with producers' co-ops on fair prices to all. As co-ops grow strong they may depart somewhat from the policy of selling at the market price. They can adopt what is called the active-price policy. They set a price which is just to all parties concerned, producers and consumers. This is the great yardstick function of the Co-operative movement. In the Sydney area they did it in turkeys last Christmas. Now, I think our time is about up.

Isadore: I am beginning to see a great light. For our

next meeting will you come out to my farm? You know
I farm a little as well as fish.

Members: Very well.

MEETING NO. 6

Topic: The Fifth Rochdale Principle—Patronage Dividends

Leader: Something tells me that all our members
will agree on the idea of a co-operative store paying
dividends to its members. That is the subject of our
discussion this evening. And as we are here at the house
of our friend Isadore perhaps we should hear from him
first.

Isadore: Gladly will I say I favor these dividends.
Anyone who has to eke out a living by a little farming
and a little fishing is no stranger to poverty. I'm anxious
to hear more about this principle.

Peter: After reserves are put aside, and also funds for
education, the earnings of the store are rebated to the
members according to the amount of their patronage.
The more you buy, the more you will get in rebate.
Many stores in the Maritimes have rebated six per cent
and higher. That is, if you have taken two hundred dollars' worth of goods in the year you will get back twelve
dollars.

Mrs. MacDaniel: How, may I ask, is this dividend to
be understood in relation to a fast growing movement
such as there is now? Should not young societies get
into a position to do a cash business with their wholesale before giving too much thought to dividends? I've
read articles to that effect.

Leader: Madam has touched upon a very important subject. I have heard experienced co-operative businessmen say that it is bad policy to rely on dividends. Dividends should not be used as organization talk, they say. Dividends do not make co-operators.

Henry: I understand that where co-operatives have grown up with the dividend idea *instead of education* there results a stunted movement. Dividend to hold membership is a most costly way. It keeps the movement drained out of funds which could be used to the greater benefit of the members by building up wholesaling facilities, for instance.

Member: Is there no advantage to be had until these wholesale facilities are built up? It seems quite some time to wait!

Leader: Oh, yes. There are several advantages to be had before the wholesale stage is reached. But some of the very greatest benefits of Co-operation come through wholesales and production. The case of Luma in Sweden is an example. When consumers in Saskatchewan went into refining oil the prices of gasoline dropped fifty per cent. There could be many other examples enumerated. Hence the desirability of having the stores build up working capital and funds for investment in the wholesale rather than place too much stress on dividends. A moderate dividend is all right. Paying a high dividend and at the same time doing business on credit with the wholesale is bad. There is no excuse for that.

Isadore: There is, I find, a great deal to learn. We grown-ups have all to go to school again, I see. I mean the study clubs. We never thought anything about these things in the past. We bought from merchants and sold to buyers as they came along and never reckoned what was happening beyond that. I guess we had our heads in a bag.

Peter: Patronage dividends shows the honesty in Co-operation—distributing the earnings to the rank and file. Millions of dollars have been put back into the hands of the people the world over in this way. In the chain store these earnings would go to capital stock and, in many cases, help to make the rich richer.

Members: And that all gives us an incentive to give our business to such an organization which we will own.

Leader: Now, we have gotten along nicely. We still have two of these important Rochdale principles to discuss at future meetings. Our next meeting will be a week from tonight.

MEETING No. 7

Topic: The Sixth Rochdale Principle—Political and Religious Neutrality

Leader: For two months we have been discussing in our circle the Rochdale principles. I see that about all our members are here tonight, and I hope comfortably seated. We are at the sixth principle—political and re-ligious neutrality. Several of our members have been studying and discussing Rochdale ideas outside of these meetings. With a thorough grasp of these principles we will be able to start and successfully operate a co-operative store here in our community. Peter, what is your understanding of this sixth principle?

Peter: When we start our store it must be run on non-denominational and non-partisan lines. We assume that our people are Christians, and running a business together should increase their goodwill for each other. We all have economic needs. It is on this ground that a common denominator is found.

Henry: I heard that in the last election some co-operators were active workers in a political party. How about that?

Peter: A man's party loyalty is his own business as long as he doesn't try to use the co-operative organization. He can speak for himself as an individual. But if he should try to commit the co-operative to the support of his party he is breaking the neutrality.

Mrs. MacDaniel: I think there is a good deal of strife over party politics, in rural communities especially. It is often a shame, I feel, to see people become bad neighbors! They really pay a big price for being divided, because they cannot buy or sell together. They have to deal with any trader that comes along. They lose so much that it becomes not worthwhile to work and produce. Hence to me any organization that will teach the people to work together regardless of their political views is a godsend!

Isadore: There is a fellow in this community who is a rank party-follower. I have heard that on nights following an election he goes braying about in front of people's houses. Can you hold a co-operative society together with such? I don't see how.

Leader: What do you think, you other members?

Mrs. MacDaniel: I think that the majority of people in a society will be different. In a group there is usually a pretty good average of common sense. Besides, one of the things we must learn before opening the door of our store, is to work together in this, even though we differ in other things. We must learn to leave our differences outside of our co-operative work.

Member: I think that going into business will help the people to get wise about depending on political parties to do everything. Someone has said that if the people can't run their own grocery store, how can they be expected to run their municipal, state, or federal governments?

Another Member: Has political neutrality always been followed by co-operatives in other countries?

Leader: No. This principle has been, so I'm told, as much honored in the breaking as in the keeping. In several countries the societies came to be used for political purposes, and suffered accordingly.

Henry: That makes it important that we understand fully this neutrality rule and follow it. Co-operation here is an economic movement. We played party politics long enough! What did it get us? I ask you.

Several Members: Hear! Hear!

Leader: Our next rally will be two weeks from to-night. In the meantime let us read and discuss these topics privately.

MEETING No. 8

Topic: The Seventh Rochdale Principle—Funds Are to Be Set Aside and Used for Education

Leader: Some time ago I talked to a man who had been a member of a co-operative store twenty years ago. The store, he said, never did well. It was in the red about all the time. It was unattractively laid out inside.

Credit was given. Bad debts piled up. The members were not loyal with their patronage. Dissatisfaction was rife.

"For three years," this man told me, "I was close to that organization. I went to all the meetings. And I never once heard of the word Rochdale." That is what the man told me.

I ask the members of this study circle what was wrong with that society?

Peter: Quite obviously it had failed to set aside funds and follow through with a program of education. I can't imagine consumers starting a store today without a thorough grounding in Rochdale principles. It is not done. Here we have been two months studying nothing else.

Isadore: If the store pays a good patronage dividend, shouldn't that keep the members loyal?

Peter: Some societies have done that. But it is not Co-operation. Experienced Co-operative managers condemn the dividend appeal. "Dividend doesn't make co-operators," they say. It makes bargain-hunters and these can never build up a co-operative system.

Mrs. MacDaniel: I have read, too, that the habit of paying high dividends is a very bad one. In new societies it tends to cut down reserves and working capital and tends to keep them down, the result being that they lack funds for expansion facilities which a growing movement will need in its wholesale and which should be financed by capital brought up from the local societies.

A Member: The method then is to build and hold a membership by means of education.

Henry: What is the best way to get the people interested? It should be quite easy to set aside a fund for education. But just how would it be spent?

Leader: There is literature. Co-operative periodicals, pamphlets, books, the use of lending libraries, study clubs are all means. The manager of a store should see to it that an attractive literature rack is set up. A committee on education should be active. It should promote meetings. Interesting speakers can be brought in. Movies are also used. After study clubs have been in action for some time, an associated study-club rally for all the clubs in a handy region can be held. This often takes the form of a social evening which includes enjoyable entertainment and singing as well as some serious enlightening talks on the wider aspects of the co-operative movement.

Mrs. MacDaniel: This is educational in another sense, for it gives people a chance to use their talents.

Henry: I think what was said a moment ago about the wider aspects of the movement is important. It seems to me that that is what makes a fundamental difference between education and dividends as a means of making people good co-operators. Education should give people the truths behind the business set-up, let the individual see himself as one of the brotherhood of man working for the common good. There are individuals born with a passion for making over the world. History shows that. Sometimes they take wrong means, such as revolution. The part of education should be to harness these to work constructively in the local community.

Leader: I fear that our time is getting short. With the reading that we have been doing at home, I feel that we now have a fair grasp of the Rochdale principles. At our next meeting we will take up details of setting up an organization. Are we all agreed that we should go ahead and found a co-operative store in this community?

Members: Agreed. Let us get started at once.

Index